The Assyrian Empire
History Nerds

AF447858

While every precaution has been taken in the preparation of this book, the publisher assumes no responsibility for errors or omissions, or for damages resulting from the use of the information contained herein.

THE ASSYRIAN EMPIRE

First edition. February 7, 2024.

Copyright © 2024 History Nerds.

ISBN: 979-8224804283

Written by History Nerds.

Also by History Nerds

Ancient Empires
The Ottoman Empire
Rome: The Rise and Fall
The Mongol Empire
The Assyrian Empire

Celtic Heroes and Legends
Celtic History
William Butler Yeats: Nobel Prize Winning Poet
Robert the Bruce
Scáthach
Finn McCool
William Wallace: Scotland's Great Freedom Fighter

Frauen des Krieges
Boudica: Königin der Icener
Jeanne d'Arc
Irena Sendler

Great Wars of the World
World War 1
World War 2
The Napoleonic Wars: One Shot at Glory
The Serbian Revolution: 1804-1835
Peace Won by the Saber: The Crimean War, 1853-1856
The Fiery Maelstrom of Freedom
The Wars of the Roses

Pirate Chronicles
Grace O'Malley: The Pirate Queen of Ireland
Blackbeard
William Kidd
Ching Shih

The History of the Vikings
Vikings
Longships on Restless Seas

Women of War
Boudica: Queen of the Iceni
Joan of Arc
Irena Sendler
Virginia Hall
Queen Amanirenas

World History
The History of the United Kingdom
The History of Ireland
The History of America
The History of Scotland
The History of Wales

Standalone
Grace O'Malley: Die Piratenkönigin von Irland

Table of Contents

The Assyrian Empire (Ancient Empires, #4) 1

Dawn of the Assyrians 4

The Rise to Power 13

Assyrian Society and Culture 25

Majestic Cities of Assyria 33

Innovations and Contributions 44

Empire at Its Zenith 55

The Decline and Fall 66

Introduction

IN THE PAGES OF THIS tome, you will unearth the secrets of an empire that once commanded the awe of the ancient world. Imagine standing in the shadow of colossal stone guardians, the Lamassu, as they watch over the procession of history itself. Can you hear the whispers of power, the clink of armor, and the murmur of scholarly debate that once echoed through the halls of Nineveh? You will trace the ascent of the Assyrians, not only through dates and decrees, but by the vibrant tales of the people who wielded iron and parchment alike. Why did the Assyrian Empire, with its unparalleled military might and administrative sophistication, crumble into the sands of time? The answers lie not only in the chronicling of battles and borders but in the understanding of human ambition and frailty. Can we learn from their triumphs and their tragedies? This book promises to be a journey across time, where the ancient stones speak, and the echoes of history reveal the blueprint of power's ascent and descent. Dare you walk the halls of vanished palaces and stand at the heart of ancient conquests? The final chapter awaits, but be warned—it holds a twist that even the mightiest of Assyrian kings could not foresee.

Embark on an intellectual odyssey that promises to enrich your understanding of the ancient world, and in doing so, shed light on the complexities of human civilization itself. Within the pages of 'The Assyrian Empire', you will not merely observe the rise and fall of a once formidable realm; you will come to grasp the very essence of power—how it is wielded, how it transforms societies, and how, ultimately, it dissipates like mist in the relentless march of time.

Imagine, for a moment, the thunderous beat of the ancient war drums heralding the approach of the Assyrian chariots. Feel the ground tremble beneath the relentless march of disciplined foot soldiers, and witness the strategic genius that birthed an empire stretching across the fertile crescent. This is not a tale pieced together from the mere fragments of archeological remains. It is a vivid tapestry woven from the threads of political intrigue, military prowess, cultural riches, and the indomitable human spirit.

You may wonder, what methods will guide us through such a labyrinthine journey of the past? The answer lies in a meticulous synthesis of historical texts, archeological discoveries, and the latest scholarly research. These will be the signposts as we traverse the ancient Near East, mapping the ebb and flow of Assyrian influence. But more than that, we will delve into the human stories—the ambitions of kings, the plights of the conquered, and the innovations of Assyrian society that still resonate today.

It is natural to meet such promises with a measure of skepticism. After all, history is too often recounted in dry, chronological recitations that fail to capture the imagination. But rest assured, this narrative is different. It breathes life into the stone reliefs and cuneiform tablets that have safeguarded Assyrian legacy for millennia. As a historian and storyteller, I am committed to peeling back the layers of time to reveal a past that is as enthralling as it is enlightening.

Picture yourself walking through the reconstructed streets of Nineveh, not as a mere spectator, but as a participant in history. Envision the transformation in your perspective as you come to understand the forces that shaped the ancient world and continue to mold our modern existence. The Assyrian Empire's story is not just one of conquest and collapse; it is a mirror reflecting the perennial human condition, the struggle for survival, significance, and legacy.

By turning each page, you solidify your commitment to uncovering the lessons an ancient empire can teach us. The value of this book is not confined to the accumulation of knowledge; it is a portal to a deeper comprehension of the cyclical nature of history and our place within it.

Dive into the depths of a bygone era where power was etched into stone and destiny was inscribed on clay tablets. Embrace the opportunity to learn not only about the Assyrians but also about the echoes of their civilization that subtly inform our present world. This is the transformative journey that 'The Assyrian Empire' invites you to undertake—a journey that promises to be as captivating as it is educational.

As the author, I extend to you the challenge to look beyond the veil of the past and discern the timeless truths hidden within. Through a narrative rich with vivid imagery and anchored in historical veracity, this book will serve as your guide through the annals of Assyrian might and majesty.

So, prepare to be transported back to an epoch where gods and kings dictated the fates of nations, and where the whispers of ancient wisdom still linger, waiting for those daring enough to listen.

Dawn of the Assyrians

Land Between Two Rivers

In the cradle of civilization, where the mighty Tigris and Euphrates rivers wind through the heart of the Middle East, an epic story unfolds—one that begins with the land itself. This land, known to the ancients as Mesopotamia, meaning "between the rivers," served as the stage upon which the Assyrian Empire would rise to power. But what was it about this stretch of earth that fostered the birth of an empire? Let us delve into the geographical significance of Mesopotamia and its indelible influence on Assyrian beginnings.

Mesopotamia was a land of paradoxes, a region that boasted both fertile plains and harsh deserts. Its defining features were the two life-giving rivers that flowed from the highlands of Armenia down to the Persian Gulf. These rivers were the arteries of Mesopotamia, carrying not just water but the very lifeblood of civilization. The annual floods brought silt and clay, which enriched the soil, making it ideal for agriculture. This abundance allowed for the sustenance of a growing population and the accumulation of wealth that would be vital for the establishment of cities and the rise of empires.

The key elements of Mesopotamia's geography included the fertile crescent, a region known for its rich soils and the birthplace of agriculture; the harsher surrounding territories, which presented both challenges and protections against invasion; and the intricate network of canals and irrigation systems engineered by its inhabitants.

But why were these geographical features so pivotal? The fertile crescent was a haven for early settlers, while the surrounding deserts and mountains served as natural fortifications. Moreover, the rivers not only nourished the land but also provided routes for trade and communication, knitting together a complex and diverse landscape into a unified whole. The Assyrians, who emerged in the northern part of Mesopotamia, would harness these geographical blessings to carve an empire that dominated the Near East.

Placing Mesopotamia within a broader framework, it was not an isolated phenomenon. Its geographical advantages were part of a larger pattern that shaped the destinies of multiple civilizations throughout history. Regions with similar endowments often rose to prominence, their rivers and fertile lands enabling the growth of powerful states and empires.

The real-world applications of Mesopotamia's geography can be seen in the way it shaped the Assyrian Empire's administrative and military strategies. The Assyrians developed a sophisticated system of governance that allowed them to control and exploit the land's resources effectively. They built roads and way stations that facilitated rapid troop movements, ensuring their military superiority.

However, common misconceptions about Mesopotamia might lead one to overlook its geographical diversity and complexity. It was not merely a land of plenty; its inhabitants faced regular challenges, such as devastating floods, which required complex solutions like advanced irrigation and flood control systems.

But what does this all mean for us today? How does the tale of a land between two rivers echo through the ages to reach us? Perhaps, it is a reminder of the enduring power of geography to shape human destiny. As much as the Assyrians were masters of their environment, they were also its children, deeply influenced by the contours of their world.

Consider this: Would the Assyrian Empire have reached such heights without the fertile plains of Mesopotamia? Would their armies have marched as far, their merchants traded as widely, their culture flourished as vibrantly? It seems unlikely. The land between the Tigris and Euphrates was not just a backdrop for the Assyrian saga; it was a character in its own right, a silent yet forceful player in the narrative of empire.

As we explore the unfolding chapters of Assyrian history, let us not forget the silent whispers of the land itself. For in the end, it is the earth beneath our feet that holds the keys to understanding the rise and fall of empires. The Assyrian Empire, with its grandeur and might, was ultimately shaped by the simple yet profound reality of the land between two rivers—a land that cradled civilization and whispered the secrets of power into the ears of those who walked upon it.

The City of Ashur

NESTLED ALONG THE WESTERN bank of the Tigris River, the city of Ashur rose from the fertile grounds of ancient Mesopotamia. It was here that the core of the Assyrian Empire was forged, its foundation stones laid in both reality and myth. The city itself was a testament to the Assyrians' indomitable spirit, a cradle of civilization that bore witness to the ebb and flow of human endeavor.

In the beginning, what was the seed from which the mighty empire sprang? The origins of Ashur are shrouded in the mists of time, but it is believed that the site was first settled by a blend of Semitic tribes, converging upon this fertile crescent, drawn by the life-giving waters of the Tigris. Could they have foreseen the lasting legacy their humble settlements would birth?

As the city grew, so did its prominence. It became a hub for trade, a crossroads for the exchange of goods, ideas, and culture. Caravans laden with textiles, spices, and rare woods wound their way through the city's gates, bringing with them the whispers of distant lands. Have you ever wondered what tales these travelers shared as they bartered their wares in the bustling marketplaces of Ashur?

Significant milestones dotted the timeline of Ashur's ascent. The city saw the rise of the Old Assyrian Kingdom around the 21st century BCE, when the first kings etched their names into history's annals. Could the stones of Ashur speak, what stories of grandeur and despair might they recount from this era of growth and conflict?

Visual aids, like the detailed bas-reliefs that once adorned the walls of the city's grand palaces, would offer a glimpse into this storied past. The images of mighty kings, divine beings, and epic battles are silent narrators of Ashur's legacy. They capture moments of triumph and tragedy, frozen in stone for eternity.

But Ashur was not a monolith; it was a tapestry of diverse influences. The city's culture evolved as it absorbed elements from neighboring regions. From the Babylonians to the south, the Assyrians inherited cuneiform writing, the vehicle for their literature, and records. How did this cultural synthesis shape the unique character of the Assyrian Empire?

In the later stages, Ashur witnessed the transition of power as the Assyrian heartland shifted north to the city of Nineveh. The changing political landscape brought new architectural marvels, but Ashur remained the spiritual nucleus, the sacred heart of the empire, revered until its eventual downfall. What does this tell us about the enduring power of sacred spaces in the human psyche?

Modern interpretations of Ashur's legacy continue to evolve. Archaeologists peel back the layers of time, uncovering artifacts and inscriptions that offer fresh perspectives on the Assyrian narrative. How do these discoveries challenge our preconceptions of ancient Assyrian society?

Yet, the journey through Ashur's past is not without its challenges and controversies. The site has seen its share of looting and destruction, particularly in recent conflicts. Such acts of desecration raise poignant questions: how do we safeguard our shared human heritage? How do we honor the memory of a civilization that shaped the world in ways still felt today?

Indeed, the city of Ashur is more than a relic of a bygone era; it is a bridge connecting past and present, a reminder of humanity's capacity for both creation and destruction. As we delve deeper into its story, let us remember that each layer of rubble and ruin was once part of a living, breathing city. The people of Ashur may have vanished into the mists of history, but their legacy endures, etched into the very fabric of civilization.

In the next chapters, we shall traverse the corridors of time, exploring the zenith and nadir of Assyrian power. We will uncover the political machinations, the military campaigns, and the intricate societal structures that underscored the empire's dominance. And through it all, the city of Ashur will stand as a silent sentinel, a beacon of the Assyrian Empire's enduring spirit. Join me on this odyssey through the annals of history, as we seek to comprehend the full magnitude of Ashur's influence on the world.

Early Dynasties

THE DAWN OF EMPIRE is often heralded by the rise of great leaders whose legacies are etched into the annals of history. The Assyrian Empire, with its might and splendor, was no different. The formative rulers and dynasties of ancient Assyria crafted the scaffold upon which a vast empire would eventually stand, reaching unprecedented heights of power and influence. It is upon their shoulders that the grandeur of the Assyrian Empire was built and through their stories that we begin to unravel the complex tapestry of this civilization's early days.

Beneath the shadow of the Zagros Mountains, the first Assyrian kings laid the foundations of a state that would grow to dominate the Near East. Little is known about these shadowy figures, their stories woven into the fabric of legend and oral tradition. Yet, through the diligent work of archaeologists and scholars, we have gleaned insights into their reigns.

The very first of these rulers, a king by the name of Tudiya, emerges from the mists of prehistory. His reign signifies the dawn of the Assyrian King List, a chronological record of kings that serves as a cornerstone for understanding Assyrian chronology. While details of his rule are scant, the mention of his name sets the stage for the lineage of kings who would follow.

Subsequent kings, such as Ushpia and Apiashal, continued to fortify the city of Ashur, establishing it as a center of trade and worship. It is from the remnants of their buildings, the inscriptions left behind, that we catch glimpses of their reigns. These early kings laid the groundwork for the political and religious institutions that would define Assyrian society for centuries to come.

With the rise of the Akkadian Empire, the first known empire in history, Assyria was drawn into a broader cultural and political sphere. The Akkadians, led by the renowned Sargon of Akkad, exerted considerable influence over the region, including the Assyrian city-states.

The Akkadian language and script became a lingua franca throughout Mesopotamia, and Assyria was no exception. The infusion of Akkadian cultural and administrative practices left an indelible mark on Assyrian governance. The Akkadian period serves as an essential chapter in the Assyrian tale, a time when the seeds of empire were sown through the exchange of ideas and the melding of cultures.

Amidst the ebb and flow of power, one figure stands tall: Shamshi-Adad I. A king of Amorite descent, his reign marked a renaissance in Assyrian history, a period when the city-states coalesced into something greater. His conquests expanded Assyrian territory, and his administrative reforms laid the blueprint for the centralized governance that would characterize later periods of Assyrian rule.

Shamshi-Adad I's letters and decrees, preserved for millennia, provide an invaluable window into the world of Assyrian politics and diplomacy. They reveal a leader adept at both war and statecraft, his legacy casting a long shadow over the generations that followed.

The Amorites, a Semitic people from the west, played a pivotal role in the development of early Assyrian civilization. Their integration into Assyrian society brought with it new ideas and traditions that enriched the cultural tapestry of the empire. Kings such as Ishme-Dagan, Shamshi-Adad I's son, continued to build upon his father's legacy, maintaining the empire's territorial gains and further refining the administration.

Archaeological evidence, including royal inscriptions and administrative texts, continues to shed light on this dynamic period. The Amorite Dynasty was a crucible in which the art of kingship was refined, setting the stage for the grandeur that was to come.

Transitioning from the early dynasties, the Middle Assyrian Period heralds an era of consolidation and expansion. It is a time characterized by robust legal codes, military prowess, and artistic achievement. Kings such as Ashur-uballit I and Tiglath-Pileser I pushed the boundaries of Assyrian influence, asserting their dominance over neighboring states and ushering in an age of empire that would endure for centuries.

The Middle Assyrian laws, a collection of legal stipulations, offer a vivid insight into the society's values and social order. Meanwhile, military annals recount the campaigns that secured Assyria's place as a regional superpower. This period encapsulates the transition from a patchwork of city-states to a centralized empire, an evolution that would define the ancient Near East.

As we trace the contours of these early dynasties, we traverse a landscape rich in history and human endeavor. The tales of these formative rulers and dynasties are not mere footnotes in the grand narrative of the Assyrian Empire; they are the bedrock upon which an entire civilization was built. Through their ambitions, their innovations, and their triumphs, we come to understand the indomitable spirit that drove the Assyrian people to carve an empire from the rugged terrain of Mesopotamia.

Trade and Economy

IN THE FERTILE CRESCENT of Mesopotamia, where the Tigris and Euphrates rivers carved their paths, the Assyrian Empire burgeoned into a civilization of staggering complexity and wealth. Cradled in this lush valley, the Assyrians developed a trade network and economic system that became the lifeblood of their empire, fueling their ascension to ancient superpower status.

Amidst this backdrop of burgeoning markets and bustling trade routes, the Assyrians emerged as masterful economic architects. The empire's internal stability, combined with its strategic geographic position, allowed it to become a nexus of international commerce.

At the heart of this economic machine were the merchants of Ashur, the central figures in the Assyrian trade narrative. These enterprising individuals were the empire's economic ambassadors, venturing beyond Assyria's borders to forge trade agreements and exchange goods in distant lands.

The core challenge they faced was the establishment of reliable and profitable trade routes across the treacherous terrain that connected the Assyrian heartland with Anatolia, the Levant, and beyond. The paths meandered through mountainous regions and arid deserts, frequented by bandits and marauding tribes. The Assyrian merchants had to navigate not only these physical hardships but also the complexities of international diplomacy.

The solution to these challenges was multifaceted. The Assyrians developed a network of roads and way stations to facilitate the movement of goods and people. They also employed a system of protective tariffs and trade agreements, ensuring that Assyrian goods—particularly textiles and tin—could be exchanged for precious metals, ivory, and other luxury items.

The results of these economic strategies were transformative. The Assyrian Empire thrived, its cities swelling with the wealth generated from trade. This wealth funded monumental building projects, military campaigns, and fostered a rich cultural environment in which the arts and sciences flourished.

As we analyze the success of Assyrian trade, it is imperative to consider its sustainability. The heavy reliance on conquest and tribute to maintain economic dominance inevitably sowed the seeds of resentment among vassal states, contributing to the empire's eventual decline.

The use of cuneiform tablets as records of transactions and treaties serves as a visual aid, illustrating the meticulousness with which the Assyrians managed their economy. These tablets bear witness to the sophistication of Assyrian bookkeeping and the importance they placed on documentation.

Reconnecting with the broader narrative of Assyrian history, the empire's economic practices were not merely a reflection of its commercial acumen but also an extension of its political might. Trade was a tool of statecraft, a means to project power, influence foreign policy, and integrate the many peoples under Assyrian dominion.

How then, did the economic practices of the Assyrians shape the political landscape of the ancient Near East? This transition thought lingers as we consider the intricate interplay between commerce and conquest, a theme that reverberates throughout the annals of history.

The Rise to Power

Military Might

In the annals of ancient history, few empires have commanded such fear and respect as that of the Assyrians. Renowned for their unyielding dominance over vast territories, it was their military might that etched their name into the stone of time. But what was the sinew and spirit of this formidable force?

At the heart of Assyrian supremacy lay a claim as bold as their renowned relief sculptures: the unparalleled effectiveness of their military strategies, weaponry, and organizational structure was the key to their expansive reign. This assertion, however, is not a mere boast of ancient chroniclers but a conclusion drawn from the concrete evidence found in archaeological excavations, contemporary accounts, and military assessments.

The primary evidence supporting this claim can be found in the meticulous records of Assyrian kings. Carved reliefs from the walls of palaces such as those in Nineveh depict scenes of sieges, illustrating the use of sophisticated siege engines like battering rams and mobile towers. These innovations enabled the Assyrians to breach the fortifications of even the most resilient cities. Moreover, the Assyrian army was one of the first to incorporate iron into their weapons, giving them a cutting edge—quite literally—over their bronze-armed adversaries.

Delving deeper into this evidence, one discovers the Assyrian military's organizational prowess. The army was divided into disciplined units with specific roles, from the fearsome cavalry to the methodical sappers who undermined city walls. The use of chariots, not merely as a noble's ride but as a strategic instrument of war, displayed their ingenuity on the battlefield. Their logistics were equally impressive, with detailed preparations ensuring a steady supply line during campaigns.

Yet, one might argue, was this military sophistication unique to the Assyrians? Counter-evidence suggests that other empires, such as the Hittites or Egyptians, also had advanced weaponry and structured military hierarchies. Some scholars point out that the Assyrian reliance on terror tactics and psychological warfare was not a measure of strength but rather a brutal approach that ultimately sowed the seeds of their downfall.

In response to this, one must consider the context of the era. Warfare was an intrinsic aspect of ancient Near Eastern societies, and the Assyrians were not the only ones to employ fear as a weapon. However, their ability to systematically integrate terror with technological and tactical innovation set them apart. Their military campaigns were not mere raids but well-planned operations aimed at achieving specific political and economic objectives.

Additional supporting evidence of Assyrian military dominance is the longevity of their empire. Despite facing numerous rebellions and external threats, the Assyrian empire maintained its dominance for centuries, a testament to its military adaptability and strategic foresight.

In conclusion, the claim of Assyrian military superiority is not without its detractors, yet when one weighs the evidence—the meticulous records, the enduring monuments, and the tales of their foes—it becomes clear that their military machine was exceptional. It was through this formidable combination of strategy, technology, and organization that the Assyrians shaped an empire that would be remembered not merely for its conquests but for the fear and awe it inspired across the ancient world. The proof of their prowess is etched in history, as enduring as the stone reliefs that glorify their triumphs. Can one then not conclude that the military might of the Assyrians was indeed the backbone of their empire, allowing them to carve out a chapter in history that still captivates scholars and laymen alike?

Conquests and Campaigns

THE ASSYRIAN EMPIRE, that great expanse of ancient Mesopotamian might, did not simply erupt into power. It was a crescendo of conquests, a symphony of strategic sieges that expanded their dominion far beyond the city-state of Ashur, from which they had sprung. Their story is one of relentless ambition, and the chapters of their military campaigns are as riveting as they are revealing.

In the earliest days, the Assyrian army was but a nascent force, primarily defensive, guarding its modest territory against neighboring tribes. It was from these small skirmishes that the seeds of empire were sown. The story begins with the ascent of Shamshi-Adad I, around 1809 BCE, who laid the foundations of what would become a military powerhouse. His conquests, though limited, set a precedent for expansion that his successors would zealously follow.

As the centuries marched on, so too did the Assyrian kings, each adding their own victories to the annals of history. The reign of Tukulti-Ninurta I (1233–1197 BCE) marked a significant military milestone when he defeated the Hittites and subjugated the Babylonians, asserting Assyrian supremacy in the region.

But it was during the Neo-Assyrian period (911–609 BCE) that the empire truly flourished. A succession of kings embarked on campaigns that would make the Assyrians the superpower of the Near East. Ashurnasirpal II (883–859 BCE) expanded the empire's borders through a series of brutal campaigns, painting the map with the blood of his enemies. His son, Shalmaneser III (858–824 BCE), continued the tradition of conquest, leaving behind a legacy etched in the famous Black Obelisk, which bears silent witness to his triumphs.

Perhaps none were more influential than Tiglath-Pileser III (745–727 BCE), whose military reforms and aggressive expansionist policies transformed the empire into a formidable force. Under his rule, the Assyrian war machine became a model of efficiency and brutality, striking fear into the hearts of its enemies.

Sargon II (722–705 BCE) and his son Sennacherib (705–681 BCE) further extended the empire's reach, with Sennacherib's siege of Jerusalem in 701 BCE becoming one of the most storied episodes of Assyrian military prowess. His destruction of the city of Babylon in 689 BCE, though ruthless, highlighted the empire's merciless approach to insubordination.

Esarhaddon (681–669 BCE) and Ashurbanipal (668–c. 631 BCE) were the last of the great Assyrian conquerors. Their campaigns into Egypt and the Levant secured Assyrian dominance, although the empire began showing signs of overextension and internal strife.

Imagine, if you will, a bas-relief carved in stone, depicting the thunderous charge of Assyrian chariots, the relentless siege of an enemy city, the disciplined formations of the infantry. These images serve as a testament to the empire's military innovations and strategies, providing a visual narrative to complement the written accounts of their conquests.

The Assyrian approach to warfare varied from region to region, adapted to the challenges presented by diverse enemies and landscapes. In the flat plains, the chariot reigned supreme, while in the mountainous highlands, infantry tactics were honed to perfection. The Assyrians were adept at exploiting the weaknesses of their foes, whether they be the fortified cities of the Babylonians or the mobile forces of the nomadic tribes.

In recent years, modern historians have revisited the campaigns of the Assyrians, bringing to light new interpretations of their military strategies. Some have posited that their success lay not only in their might but also in their ability to assimilate and adapt the best practices of those they conquered.

Yet, the Assyrian penchant for brutality and the reliance on fear as a tool of war invited resistance and rebellion. The empire's overreach and the eventual rise of new powers, such as the Medes and Babylonians, precipitated a turning point. The fall of Nineveh in 612 BCE marked the end of the Assyrian Empire, and with it, the cessation of their storied campaigns.

Was their downfall a consequence of their own hubris? A destiny written in the blood they so liberally spilled? These are questions that scholars continue to debate. But one cannot deny the indelible mark left by the Assyrians, whose conquests and campaigns shaped the course of history, leaving behind a legacy as intricate and formidable as the reliefs on their palace walls. The Assyrian Empire, through its military might, created an epoch that, though vanished, still echoes through time. And in the contemplation of their rise and fall, one must wonder: what lessons do their conquests hold for the empires of today, and for those yet to come?

The Art of Diplomacy

IN THE SHADOW OF SUCH military might, it is easy to overlook the more subtle instruments of power wielded by the Assyrian Empire. Yet, in the grand tapestry of their history, the threads of diplomacy, marriage alliances, and tribute are interwoven with the more vivid hues of conquest and subjugation. To focus solely on the latter is to miss the nuances that allowed the empire to craft a vast, interconnected web of control that transcended the battlefield.

Beneath the Assyrian sun, the city of Ashur bustled with not just the clamor of commerce but also with the whispered negotiations of envoys and the soft footsteps of royal brides crossing borders to bind nations. These were the sinews that held the empire together as much as any siege engine or chariot.

The case of the marriage alliance between the Assyrian Empire and the kingdom of Babylonia in the 8th century BCE serves as a particularly striking example. King Sargon II, whose armies had thundered across the Near East, was also a master of the softer arts of empire.

The Babylonian kingdom, though weakened by internal strife and the pressure of Assyrian military campaigns, still held significant cultural and religious influence in the region. It was an entity that could not merely be crushed without risking the ire of other states and the gods themselves. The challenge for Sargon II was to assert Assyrian dominance while maintaining the semblance of Babylonian autonomy—a delicate balance of power and perception.

The solution lay in a strategic marriage alliance. Sargon's son, Sennacherib, was united in matrimony with the Babylonian princess Naqi'a. This alliance was a masterstroke of diplomacy, for it secured a blood tie between the two royal houses, placating the Babylonian populace and clergy with the idea that their traditions and autonomy were being respected, even as Assyrian influence seeped deeper into their society.

The results were telling. While rebellions and unrest were not entirely quelled, the marriage created a significant deterrent against insurrection, as any revolt against Assyria was now also a revolt against a queen with Babylonian blood. Furthermore, it afforded the Assyrians a greater influence in Babylonian affairs without the need for constant military intervention.

Reflecting on this union, it becomes apparent that the Assyrians understood the power of perception and the importance of cultural sensitivity in maintaining an empire. It was not enough to conquer; one must also convince the conquered of their place in the larger narrative of Assyrian supremacy.

Yet, this strategy did not come without its criticisms. Some in the Assyrian court viewed such alliances as unnecessary entanglements, potential threats to the purity of the Assyrian lineage, and a sign of weakness. Others, however, saw them as a necessary evolution of statecraft in an ever-more complex political landscape.

This episode of Assyrian diplomacy is but one thread in the complex weave of their imperial fabric. It demonstrates how the empire's reach extended beyond the battlefield and into the bedchambers and council rooms of their adversaries. The marriage of Sennacherib and Naqi'a was a microcosm of a strategy replicated with various other states and on numerous occasions.

How did this influence the broader narrative of the Assyrian Empire's expansion and consolidation of power? It is clear that while the empire is often remembered for its military prowess, its longevity and stability also depended on its ability to adapt and employ a wide array of statecraft tools.

As we close the chapter on this instance of Assyrian diplomacy, one must ponder: How might modern states learn from the Assyrian example? In an era of global interdependence, could it be that the ancient arts of marriage alliances and the careful weaving of political ties are due for a resurgence?

Indeed, the Assyrian Empire's story is not simply one of conquest but also one of connection—of binding the fates of disparate peoples into a single narrative of power. And so, we must ask ourselves: What other aspects of Assyrian diplomacy remain buried, awaiting discovery, to further enlighten our understanding of their empire? As history whispers its secrets, it is our task to listen and learn.

Gods and Kings

THE ASSYRIAN EMPIRE, a colossal mosaic of territories and cultures, stood not solely on the might of its warriors but also on a divine mandate believed to be ordained by the heavens. The elaborate tapestry of this ancient civilization was intricately woven with threads of theology and monarchy, where gods and kings sat in the closest communion, each reinforcing the other's authority.

At the heart of the Assyrian expansion was the principle of divine right, which the monarchs wielded with astute understanding and unyielding conviction. The kings, anointed as earthly representatives of the gods, embarked upon campaigns of conquest and consolidation, believing their victories to be a fulfillment of celestial will. This spiritual justification was paramount, not as mere superstition, but as a robust pillar of imperial policy, suffusing every military endeavor with holy purpose.

The pantheon of Assyrian deities, led by Ashur, the supreme god, was seen as an active force in the empire's destiny. Temples soared as beacons of power, and the rituals performed within their hallowed walls were as much a display of piety as they were of political propaganda. The link between the divine and the earthly rule was not a subtle nuance but a blatant declaration of the king's right to rule over the vast stretches of land and diverse peoples.

Consider, for example, the reign of Tiglath-Pileser III, a ruler whose military campaigns brought vast swathes of the Near East under Assyrian dominion. His annals speak not just of tactical brilliance but also of divine favor. He frequently invoked Ashur's name, claiming that it was the god who 'opened the lands' to him and 'subdued the hostile kings.' Here, the narrative crafted by the king was unequivocal: his conquests were as much a divine commission as they were a matter of statecraft.

This seamless blend of religion and royal ambition was further demonstrated in the practice of erecting stelae and monuments inscribed with tales of conquest. These inscriptions, often embellished with rich, vibrant imagery, served a dual purpose. They immortalized the king's achievements and underscored the gods' endorsement of his rule. One such stele depicts Ashurnasirpal II, resplendent and larger than life, with gods hovering above, bestowing upon him the symbols of rulership—a clear message that his authority was heaven-sent.

From another angle, the empire's religious infrastructure played a critical role. The priesthood, a powerful entity within Assyrian society, operated in tandem with the monarchy. The prophets and diviners held considerable influence, their oracles and interpretations of omens guiding the king's decisions. In moments of doubt, it was the priestly cast that provided the divine confirmation necessary for the king to act.

Moreover, the Assyrian practice of relocating vanquished peoples served not only a strategic purpose but also a theological one. By integrating these populations into the Assyrian heartland, the empire not only diffused potential rebellions but also spread the worship of Assyrian gods, further legitimizing their dominion.

Data from archaeological findings and ancient texts provide substantial evidence of this divine mandate. The annals of kings are replete with references to gods leading the armies, granting victories, and commanding the subjugation of foreign lands. This intertwining of faith and policy was a masterful stroke of governance, ensuring that the populace, both Assyrian and subjugated, recognized the divine underpinnings of the empire's expansionist policies.

However, not all accepted this narrative without skepticism. Within the empire, there were likely those who questioned the convenience of divine endorsement for earthly ambitions. Yet, such dissent was rarely documented, overshadowed by the dominant narrative of divine right that the Assyrian state machinery propagated.

To clarify complex terms, one must understand that 'divine right' in this context was not a mere religious concept but a political tool, a means by which the Assyrian kings solidified their rule and justified their actions. It was a doctrine that blurred the lines between the celestial and the terrestrial, making the king's word law and his actions, the will of the gods.

In conclusion, the role of religion and the divine right in the Assyrian Empire was not a peripheral detail but a central tenet of its existence. The conquests were not merely territorial ambitions; they were holy crusades. This potent combination of religious fervor and royal authority was a driving force behind the Assyrian Empire's expansion, a fact that is crucial to our understanding of this ancient civilization's history.

Infrastructure and Administration

IN THE SHADOW OF DIVINE right and celestial mandate, the Assyrian Empire's expansion was not merely a conquest of lands but also a venture in creating a sustainable system that could support such a vast domain. The empire, a complex network of cities and provinces, required a robust infrastructure and a meticulous administrative apparatus to maintain its territorial integrity and facilitate its growth. The Assyrian kings, aware of this necessity, invested in the development of roads and devised administrative practices with the same vigor they applied to their military campaigns. The logistics that supported an empire were as crucial as the spears and shields of its soldiers.

Imagine embarking on a journey through the Assyrian heartland. What would be essential for such an endeavor? The answer lies in the intricate network of roads that crisscrossed the empire, a testament to Assyrian engineering and foresight. These roads enabled not just the movement of armies but also the flow of trade, communication, and administration—arteries of the empire pulsing with life and activity.

A broad overview of this vast system reveals a multi-layered approach. It includes the construction of thoroughfares, the establishment of waystations and postal systems, and the implementation of a bureaucracy that could oversee such operations. The Assyrian road system was not a random web of pathways but a structured and deliberate project aimed at connecting the empire's many facets.

Delve deeper, and one will discover the immense labor and coordination required to build these roads. They were often paved, marked with milestones, and patrolled by guards to ensure the safety of travelers and the swift passage of official messengers. The waystations, strategically placed at regular intervals, provided rest and resupply points for both man and beast. The postal system, an innovation in its own right, utilized relays of horses and riders to carry messages across vast distances with remarkable speed.

But what about the men who managed these feats? Enter the Assyrian administrative practices. A complex hierarchy of officials, from provincial governors to local scribes, ensured the smooth running of the empire. They collected taxes, maintained census records, and administered justice. They were the unseen hands that kept the Assyrian machine well-oiled and functioning.

Here's a practical piece of advice: to understand the scale of Assyrian administration, one must consider the meticulous nature of their record-keeping. Clay tablets, unearthed by archaeologists, reveal the precision with which the Assyrians managed their empire. These documents contain everything from trade transactions to military logistics, offering a window into the day-to-day operations that sustained Assyrian dominance.

How can we validate the effectiveness of such systems? The proof lies in the longevity and stability of the Assyrian Empire. It thrived for centuries, not just because of its military might but also due to its ability to administer and sustain its vast territories.

Troubleshooting, however, was an integral part of the Assyrian administrative process. Revolts and corruption were ever-present threats to the empire's stability. The Assyrians responded with a policy of swift and often brutal retribution to deter rebellion, coupled with a network of spies and informants to root out corruption before it could spread.

The empire, in its zenith, was a marvel of ancient world logistics, but this did not happen without foresight and adaptation. The Assyrians learned from their challenges and continually refined their infrastructure and administration, understanding that the strength of an empire lay as much in its organizational capabilities as in its armies.

In summary, the Assyrian Empire's road networks and administrative practices were not merely functional necessities; they were the sinews and bones that held the empire together. As we delve into the annals of history, we witness an empire that understood the value of strong foundations. The Assyrian tale of infrastructure and administration is one of human ingenuity and the relentless pursuit of order amidst the chaos of expansion.

Now, consider this: in what ways does our modern society mirror the Assyrian approach to infrastructure and governance? Perhaps, in the shadow of our highways, administrative buildings, and postal services, we walk a path not so different from that of the ancient Assyrians. Could it be that our contemporary world, with its complex systems and bureaucracies, is built upon the principles pioneered by an empire that rose and fell millennia ago?

In the grand narrative of the Assyrian Empire, we find not only a story of conquest and divine right but also one of innovation and administration—a narrative where kings and officials worked hand in hand to construct an infrastructure that would stand the test of time. The Assyrian legacy, therefore, is not solely etched in the annals of military triumphs but also in the silent stones of the roads that once connected an empire and in the clay tablets that chronicled its existence.

Assyrian Society and Culture

Daily Life in the Empire

Amidst the bustling streets of Nineveh, the heart of the Assyrian Empire, a potter named Ashur-nasir carefully shapes the clay on his wheel, his skilled hands breathing life into the earth as the sun begins its descent. The chatter of the marketplace surrounds him, a cacophony of haggling voices, braying donkeys, and the distant clang of metal from the smith's forge. The city thrives as a hub of culture and commerce, its grandeur a testament to the might of the empire.

Ashur-nasir and his family represent the backbone of Assyrian society—the commoners, whose labor and ingenuity fuel the empire's vast economy. Yet, not far from his modest workshop stands the imposing palace of a high-ranking official, a stark reminder of the societal chasm between commoner and elite.

The challenges faced by Ashur-nasir and his kin are manifold. Toiling long hours to meet the demands of both the local community and the state, they must balance the need for survival with the oppressive taxes levied by imperial decree. The strategies to cope are as varied as the products of their labor. Some, like Ashur-nasir, dedicate themselves to mastering a trade, while others form collectives to share resources and knowledge, ensuring no single family bears the brunt of a bad season.

Despite these hurdles, the results of their tenacity are evident in the thriving markets, the quality of their crafts, and the resilience of their communities. They have woven a social fabric strong enough to withstand the pressures of empire, yet supple enough to adapt to its ever-changing demands.

Upon reflection, the lives of these commoners offer a rich tapestry of experience and insight. Their persistent innovation in the face of adversity reveals a deep-seated understanding of both their craft and their society. Critics might argue that their contributions are too often overshadowed by the monumental achievements of the empire's ruling class, but without the foundation of their labor, the grandiose structures of Assyria would crumble to dust.

To truly grasp the daily life within this ancient empire, it is essential to consider the visuals of urban and rural existence. Imagine the contrast between the austere mud-brick homes of the commoners and the ornate palaces of the elite, adorned with reliefs depicting gods and conquests. Picture the vast fields surrounding the cities, where peasants toil under the watchful eye of Ashur, the god of the state, hoping for a bountiful harvest to appease both deity and king.

These individual stories, like that of Ashur-nasir, are but threads in the larger narrative of the Assyrian Empire. They serve as reminders that the grandeur of an empire is not solely measured by its conquests or the wealth of its rulers, but also by the everyday lives of its people. Their struggles, successes, and social structures are integral to understanding the true nature of Assyrian civilization.

As the stars begin to pepper the twilight sky and Ashur-nasir sets his tools aside, one might wonder what dreams occupy his thoughts. Does he aspire for his children to rise above the station of their birth, or does he find contentment in the rhythm of his craft? Could the empire endure without the silent strength of its commoners, or are they the unseen bedrock upon which all else is built? As we leave this thought, let us ponder this: In the grand tapestry of history, whose hands are truly shaping the course of empires—the powerful few or the laboring many?

Art and Architecture

IN THE SHADOWS OF GRAND palaces and amidst the echoes of conquest, the Assyrian Empire carved its legacy into the annals of history not just through the might of its armies but also via the splendor of its artistic and architectural innovations. The distinctiveness of Assyrian art and architecture lies in their profound ability to convey the empire's ideals and the everyday life of its people.

Why, one may ask, is there a need to juxtapose the artistry and construction prowess of a civilization long crumbled to dust? The answer, as clear as the bas-reliefs on an Assyrian wall, is to glean insights into a culture's identity, values, and technological advancements. By examining the contours of stone reliefs and the grandeur of ziggurats, one can decipher the narrative of a people who valued power, spirituality, and the immortalization of their achievements.

For our analytical expedition, let us set the criteria: the depiction of deities and royalty, the use of space and scale, and the technological ingenuity of construction. Through these benchmarks, we shall explore the common threads woven into the fabric of Assyrian art and architecture, while also unraveling the strands of their distinctiveness.

Consider, if you will, the artistry of the Assyrian bas-relief. These intricate carvings, found on the limestone walls of monumental structures, share a common theme: the glorification of the king and the gods. Kings are often depicted as larger-than-life figures, towering over their enemies and their own subjects—a visual assertion of their divine mandate to rule. The Assyrian gods, too, are grandly portrayed, providing a celestial endorsement of the king's authority. Does this not reveal a society where power and piety are inextricably intertwined?

Yet, within these carvings, one also discerns a striking contrast. The detailed attire and regalia of the royalty stand in stark relief against the simplistic representation of the commoners. This disparity accentuates the social hierarchy, portraying the ruling class as not only mighty but also as the chosen intermediaries between the divine and the earthly realms.

Moving from the walls to the wider stage of Assyrian architecture, one beholds the ziggurat—a structure that physically and symbolically reaches towards the heavens. These tiered temples stood as a testament to both the religious devotion of the Assyrians and their architectural prowess. By replicating the mountainous abode of their gods, the Assyrians sought to bring the divine closer to the terrestrial.

And what of the palaces, with their imposing walls and gates guarded by colossal lamassu statues? These winged bulls with the heads of men serve as both protectors and symbols of power. The sheer scale of these edifices and their guardians is a direct reflection of the empire's might and a clear message to both subjects and visitors alike: here lies an unstoppable force.

Yet, in contrast, the commoners' dwellings were modest, often constructed from mud-brick, a material far less enduring than the limestone of royal buildings. This architectural dichotomy not only reflects the disparity in wealth but also in the legacy left behind—stone endures, while mud-brick erodes, much like the memory of the common man compared to that of the king.

Delving deeper into these comparisons, we uncover broader implications: the Assyrians' art and architecture were tools of statecraft, designed to impress upon all the power of the empire and the divine right of its rulers. They were also enduring records of their achievements, meant to outlast the empire itself.

Now, consider our modern constructions and artistic expressions. Are they not also reflections of our values and hierarchies, just as the Assyrians' were of theirs? The towering skyscrapers of today's metropolises, the monuments to our leaders—do they not echo the same desires for legacy and the same assertions of power?

In the solitude of contemplation, one might ask: What truly endures? Is it stone or spirit? The grandeur of the Assyrian Empire lives on not merely through its physical remnants but through the indelible mark it left on human culture.

Language and Literature

THROUGHOUT THE ASSYRIAN Empire's history, language and literature stand out as threads of undeniable significance. These elements not only served as the vessels of communication and cultural continuity but also as the canvas upon which the Assyrians painted the portrait of their intellectual prowess. As we unfurl the scroll of Assyrian scholarship, we find that two languages, Akkadian and Aramaic, were central to the empire's administrative, literary, and cultural narratives.

The Assyrian Empire's linguistic landscape was as varied as it was vibrant. Within this expanse, the importance of Akkadian and Aramaic cannot be overstated, for they were the sinews and bones of Assyrian written expression. Alongside these linguistic giants stood a rich tradition of literature that both reflected and shaped the world from which it sprang.

Akkadian: The Language of Empires

Akkadian, an ancient Semitic tongue, was the lingua franca of Assyria and the broader Mesopotamian civilization. It was not merely a means of communication but a powerful tool that united disparate peoples under Assyrian rule. The cuneiform script in which it was written remains one of the most enduring symbols of ancient literacy.

The corpus of Akkadian literature is vast, encompassing epic poetry, legal documents, and diplomatic correspondence. Texts such as the Epic of Gilgamesh not only provide us with thrilling narratives but also offer a window into the values and beliefs of the time. The Akkadian language, with its complex grammar and extensive vocabulary, was capable of expressing nuanced thought and emotion, which the Assyrians harnessed to great effect.

Aramaic: The Vernacular of the Common People

As the empire expanded, Aramaic emerged as the vernacular of choice for the everyday Assyrian. This Semitic language, with its alphabetic script, was more accessible than the cuneiform of Akkadian, leading to its adoption as the official language in the later years of the empire.

Aramaic's significance is underscored by the fact that it was the language of the people, used for trade, administration, and personal correspondence. It is from Aramaic that we have inherited a wealth of documents that reveal the day-to-day life of the Assyrians, from mundane transaction records to heartfelt personal letters.

The Literary Contributions of the Assyrians

The Assyrians were not merely passive inheritors of a literary tradition; they were active contributors to it. They took the raw materials of words and crafted them into forms that continue to inspire awe and wonder. The Assyrian literature, much like their monumental architecture, was an expression of their identity and power.

The library of Ashurbanipal in Nineveh, with its thousands of clay tablets, stands as a testament to the Assyrian commitment to knowledge and scholarship. It was here that scribes compiled and copied literary works, preserving them for posterity. The influence of Assyrian literature can be seen in its impact on neighboring cultures and its survival into the modern world.

As we traverse from the grandeur of past empires to the present, let us ask: How do the languages and literatures of ancient civilizations inform our own linguistic journey? How does the preservation of texts from antiquity enrich our understanding of human history and thought?

In the silence between the turning of pages, one might ponder the weight of words and the permanence of ink. The legacy of the Assyrian Empire, etched onto clay tablets and written in the annals of literary history, endures as a narrative of human creativity and resilience.

Laws and Justice

AMIDST THE SWIRLING sands of time and the relentless march of empires, there lies the formidable expanse of the Assyrian domain. A civilization of meticulous administrators and fearsome warriors, the Assyrians forged a legacy that has echoed through the ages. To grasp the full extent of their might, one must not only admire their towering ziggurats and relentless campaigns but also delve into the intricate web of laws and justice that sustained their society.

Transport yourself to the ancient city of Nineveh, vibrant and bustling under the rule of a king like Hammurabi, whose own code predated Assyria's zenith. Imagine the reverberation of the crier's voice in the marketplace, announcing the edicts that would govern daily life. This was a society where order was paramount, and the law was both sword and shield in the hands of the state.

Historical milestones in the evolution of Assyrian law reveal a system that was both strict and sophisticated. The Middle Assyrian Laws, a collection from around 1076 BCE, showcase a society deeply concerned with property rights, marriage contracts, and personal injury cases. These laws were not merely punitive; they offered a structure through which the empire could administer its vast territories. They addressed issues from the mundane to the monumental, reflecting an understanding that justice was the bedrock upon which the stability of the empire rested.

Yet, how does this ancient legal framework relate to our modern sensibilities and challenges? The echoes of Assyrian legal principles can be heard in our own quest for justice and order. Property rights, contractual obligations, and penal codes remain central to our legal systems, a testament to the enduring influence of ancient jurisprudence.

Why does this history matter now? In a world replete with conflict and disparity, the pursuit of justice remains a universal theme. The Assyrian Empire's experience reminds us that the rule of law is fundamental to the governance of a society, ensuring fairness and mitigating chaos. By studying their legal systems, we gain insight into how our own can be refined and adapted to meet contemporary needs.

As we transition from the grand narrative of Assyrian dominance to the more intimate corridors of their societal workings, we glimpse the everyday lives of those who lived under the shadow of Ashurbanipal's might. Each decree, etched in cuneiform, each judgment handed down by the king or his appointees, was a thread in the fabric of Assyrian life.

Consider the plight of a commoner, aggrieved by a neighbor's encroachment on his field. In the Assyrian legal system, such a dispute would be settled through established protocols, demonstrating that even in an empire renowned for its military prowess, there was space for the grievances of the individual to be heard.

As we delve deeper into the details, we find that Assyrian law was not a monolith. It was a living, breathing organism that evolved with the empire. The laws that governed a trade agreement were as meticulously crafted as the strategies that won battles. In this complex network of statutes and penalties, one glimpses the silhouette of the modern-day legal system, with its multifaceted approach to governance.

How often do we consider the lineage of our own laws? Do we recognize the ancient foundations upon which our societal order is built? The narrative of Assyrian law compels us to reflect on the origins of our own legal principles and the ways in which they have been shaped by millennia of human experience.

In the silence of a courtroom or the clamor of a legislative debate, one might discern the distant whispers of Assyrian magistrates and scholars. Their quest for order and equity was not so different from our own. The legacy of the Assyrian Empire, with its codes and decrees, continues to serve as a narrative of humanity's enduring search for a just society.

Majestic Cities of Assyria

Nimrud: A Capital Reborn

Once a heartbeat in the vast body of the Assyrian Empire, the city of Nimrud lay shrouded in the mists of time, its stories buried under the earth, awaiting the touch of the future to breathe life into its ancient walls once again. It was a city that had seen the zenith of power, the despair of ruin, and the curious gaze of rediscovery. But what secrets did it clutch to its chest along the banks of the Tigris River?

In its earliest whisperings, Nimrud was not the grand capital one might imagine. It was but one of many modest settlements dotting the fertile crescent, a cradle of civilization. The city's inception, lost to the echoes of millennia, was humble, a place where the seeds of empire were unwittingly sown.

As the centuries unfurled like the fronds of a date palm, so too did the stature of Nimrud. Ashurnasirpal II, in a move of strategic genius and royal ambition, established it as the capital in the ninth century BCE. The city burgeoned, its borders expanding as if drawing breath for the very first time. Palaces and temples soared towards the heavens, bedecked with reliefs that whispered tales of gods and kings. The air was thick with the scent of cedar from Lebanon, and the clatter of commerce filled the streets.

As the empire expanded, regional variations in Nimrud's influence became apparent. In the far reaches of the empire, the city was a distant beacon of power, a symbol rather than a tangible presence. To those within its immediate sphere, Nimrud was the center of the world, a place where policy was made, and fortunes were won or lost.

The passage of time eventually saw the waning of the Assyrian Empire, and with it, the decline of Nimrud. Invading forces, the ebb and flow of power, and the relentless grind of time buried the once resplendent city beneath layers of dust and obscurity. How could such a pinnacle of human achievement simply vanish from the annals of history?

Modern interpretations of Nimrud, fueled by its rediscovery in the 19th century, have sparked a renewed interest in the Assyrian legacy. Archaeologists, like Austen Henry Layard, delved into the soil with fervor, uncovering the long-lost city. With each artifact unearthed, Nimrud's story was pieced back together, a mosaic of history slowly reassembling from the fragments left behind.

Yet, Nimrud's tale is not without its challenges and controversies. Debates have raged over the interpretation of its texts and the significance of its relics. The city has also faced modern threats, such as looting and deliberate destruction, which have endangered its survival. These events marked turning points, rallying the global community to preserve and protect this irreplaceable window into the past.

Nimrud, in its rebirth, has become a poignant symbol of the fragility of cultural heritage. It stands as a stark reminder that the threads of history are delicate and easily severed by the hands of time and turmoil.

"Can we ever truly capture the essence of Nimrud?" one might ponder. The relics and ruins offer silent narratives, but the full depth of its pulse—its people, their whispers, and the weight of their footsteps—can only be imagined.

A city reborn, Nimrud continues to captivate, to inspire awe, and to provoke questions about our place in the long, winding tapestry of human endeavor. It is a testament to the enduring desire to seek out our origins, to understand the legacies left behind by those who walked before us. In the end, isn't that the quest at the heart of all history? To look into the face of the past and see reflected in it both the dawn and the dusk of empires?

Nineveh: The Heart of Assyria

AMIDST THE ROLLING tapestry of the ancient Near East, where the Tigris and Euphrates rivers entwine like serpents, there lies the remnants of a city that was once the very soul of an empire. Nineveh, the heart of Assyria, stands as a testament to the might and majesty that was the Assyrian Empire. Its ruins whisper of past glories and forgotten dreams, but if we listen closely, we can still discern the echoes of its grandeur and the pulse of its immense power.

Imagine, if you will, the bustling streets of Nineveh in its heyday. The air is rich with the scent of spices and the clamor of a myriad of languages as traders from distant lands mingle with the local populace. Towering gates adorned with fearsome deities guard the city, and within its walls, grand palaces and temples reach toward the heavens, their intricate reliefs chronicling the deeds of gods and monarchs. What tales might these ancient stones recount if they could speak?

The central figures of our story are the Assyrian emperors, divine in their rule, each contributing to Nineveh's splendor. Their legacies are etched not only in stone but in the very fabric of the city's existence. Sennacherib, for instance, expanded the city's boundaries and erected the famous Hanging Gardens, reputed to be a wonder of the world, although some scholars argue they were located in Babylon. His son, Esarhaddon, continued the expansion and consolidation of Assyrian power, ensuring Nineveh's position as the empire's crown jewel.

Yet, despite the grandeur, Nineveh faced challenges, both external and internal. The empire's reach provoked resentment and rebellion among subjugated peoples, while court intrigues and succession crises threatened stability from within. The problem was as old as empire itself: how to maintain control over vast territories with diverse populations, and how to ensure the continuity of power through the unpredictable tides of fate and fortune.

The approach to these challenges was multifaceted. The Assyrians deployed military might and strategic alliances, but they also engaged in psychological warfare, with terrifying depictions of their power and brutality. They developed sophisticated administrative systems to manage their territories and used cultural assimilation as a tool for integration. The results were a complex blend of control that allowed Nineveh to flourish as the imperial capital, its influence radiating throughout the Near East.

The results, as seen through the archaeological record, were staggering. Nineveh was transformed into one of the largest cities of its time, an epicenter of culture and power. Its libraries housed thousands of clay tablets, preserving the knowledge of the ancient world. The city's gardens and aqueducts were engineering marvels that showcased the empire's understanding of both beauty and utility.

Yet, we must analyze and reflect upon these achievements within the broader context of their impact. Assyrian rule was often harsh, and their military campaigns left a trail of destruction. The empire's reliance on fear as a means of control begs the question of the ethical cost of such grandeur. Can splendor justify the suffering it may have been built upon?

As we connect these insights to the broader narrative of Assyrian history, we see Nineveh not as an isolated phenomenon but as a pivotal chapter in the story of civilization. Its influence extended far beyond its walls, shaping the political, cultural, and economic landscapes of the ancient world.

And now, as we stand amidst the scattered stones of what was once a bustling metropolis, one cannot help but wonder: what lessons can we draw from Nineveh's tale? How does its rise and fall inform our understanding of power, culture, and the delicate balance that civilizations must strike to endure?

Nineveh's story is a mirror reflecting the brilliance and the brittleness of empire. It reminds us that the grandest of cities can fade into obscurity, leaving behind only fragments for future generations to piece together. But it also assures us that these fragments can speak across the ages, urging us to remember and to learn.

What, then, will be the legacy of our own civilizations? Will the echoes of our achievements resonate through the corridors of time as Nineveh's have, or will they too be buried beneath the sands, whispers of a bygone era waiting to be unearthed by the curious and the brave?

Khorsabad: Sargon's Legacy

IN THE SHADOW OF THE monumental legacy of Nineveh, another city rises from the annals of history, beckoning us to explore its storied past. Khorsabad, less known yet equally enthralling, stands as a testament to the ambition and vision of one particular Assyrian ruler: Sargon II. Here, in this ancient metropolis, the threads of history weave a tale of grandeur, innovation, and the ceaseless pursuit of immortality through stone and conquest.

Step through the mists of time to the eighth century BCE, a pivotal era when the Assyrian Empire was reaching the zenith of its power. Picture a ruler, Sargon II, ascending to the throne amidst political turmoil and usurpation. His name, echoing that of the legendary Sargon of Akkad, was a declaration, a promise to resurrect past glories and forge an empire that would eclipse all that came before.

What drives a man to build an entire city from the dust? Is it the lust for power, the fear of mortality, or the unyielding grip of destiny? As we peel back the layers of history, we find that Khorsabad, known to the ancients as Dur-Sharrukin, "Sargon's Fortress," was an embodiment of royal propaganda, a physical manifestation of the divine right to rule, and a bold statement etched into the landscape of the ancient world.

Sargon's reign, marked by military campaigns that expanded the empire's borders, was also distinguished by his ambitious building projects. Khorsabad was to be his pièce de résistance, a new capital designed to reflect the might and sophistication of Assyria. Every brick laid and every colossus erected served a singular vision—to immortalize Sargon's name and establish a legacy that would endure through the ages.

But what did it truly mean to build such a city? Beyond the towering ziggurat that pierced the heavens, the sprawling palaces, and the protective walls that stretched like the arms of giants, Khorsabad was a marvel of urban planning and engineering. Aqueducts channeled water from distant mountains, gardens bloomed with exotic flora, and the city's layout was a testament to the empire's advancements in science and mathematics.

Does the grandeur of Khorsabad's ruins resonate with us today? In a world where cities rise and fall, where the pursuit of legacy is often entangled with the political machinations of the powerful, Khorsabad's story is strikingly relevant. It serves as a reflection on leadership, the responsibilities of power, and the impermanence of human endeavors.

As we delve deeper into the narrative of Khorsabad, we are compelled to ask: What can we learn from Sargon's ambition? Can the echoes of his legacy help us navigate the complexities of our own time, or are they merely cautionary tales warning us of hubris and the fleeting nature of power?

Khorsabad was not merely a city of bricks and mortar; it was a hub of culture and learning, a place where scribes recorded the knowledge of the day onto clay tablets, where artisans and craftsmen honed their skills, and where the rituals of religion and governance were performed under the watchful eyes of deities carved into the limestone walls.

Yet, for all its splendor, Khorsabad was a human endeavor, with all the inherent flaws and vulnerabilities. The city, barely completed before Sargon's death, was ultimately abandoned by his successors, its purpose unfulfilled. What does this tell us about the intentions of men and the forces of history that so often disrupt the grandest of plans?

In a single, poignant line, the fate of Khorsabad encapsulates the ephemeral nature of human ambition: The city, conceived in power, was relinquished to the sands of time.

As we stand amidst Khorsabad's ruins today, the once-mighty city offers us a canvas upon which to project our understanding of the ancient world. Its legacy, though overshadowed by the more enduring Nineveh, is no less significant. In its silence, it speaks volumes about the Assyrian Empire, the vision of one king, and the relentless march of time that claims all empires, great and small.

What, then, are we to make of Sargon's legacy? Does it serve as a warning, a lesson, or an inspiration? Can the stones of Khorsabad still shape the world of today, or have they relinquished their voice to the annals of history?

Arbela: A Center of Worship

ARBELA, KNOWN TODAY as Erbil, stands as a beacon of spiritual significance in the history of the Assyrian Empire. This ancient city, a cradle of civilization, bore witness to the fervent prayers and rituals that permeated the very soul of Assyria. Though eclipsed in political prominence by cities such as Nineveh, Arbela's religious stature was unparalleled, and its impact on the Assyrian identity remains a subject of profound intrigue.

At the heart of Arbela's enduring legacy was the temple of Ishtar, the Assyrian goddess of love and war. Her worship was not merely a facet of daily life; it was the cornerstone of Assyrian spirituality, that sought to galvanize the empire's people against the tides of time and invasion.

The claim here is clear: Arbela was not just a city of worship; it was the spiritual engine of the Assyrian Empire, a place where their divine and mortal realms sought to intertwine, to create a powerful narrative of identity and continuity.

The primary evidence for Arbela's preeminence lies in the accounts of ancient historians and in the archaeological record. Tablets and inscriptions unearthed from the soil of this storied city speak of grand processions, of sacrifices made in the name of Ishtar, and of oracles that guided kings and commoners alike. These tangible remnants serve as silent testimonies to the fervor and devotion that once pervaded Arbela's sacred precincts.

Delving deeper into this evidence, we encounter the words of Herodotus, who chronicled the significance of Arbela in his Histories. He writes of the mystique surrounding the city's oracles, suggesting that the very fate of the empire was often seen as resting in the hands of the divine, as interpreted by the priestesses of Ishtar. The prominence of these rituals in the collective psyche of the Assyrians cannot be overstated; they were not mere religious formalities but pivotal events that shaped policies and destinies.

Yet, one must also consider counter-evidence that emerges from the broader historical context. Some scholars posit that the religious centrality of Arbela may have been somewhat overstated, suggesting that its influence waxed and waned with the political and military fortunes of the empire. Could the city's significance have been magnified by later generations, who looked back with nostalgia on the days of Assyria's greatness?

In response to such skepticism, further clarification is warranted. The enduring veneration of Ishtar, whose cult persisted even beyond the fall of the empire, lends weight to the argument that Arbela's religious influence was more than mere happenstance. The continuity of her worship, as evidenced by the survival of temples and iconography dedicated to her, underscores the city's pivotal role in perpetuating Assyrian religious tradition.

Moreover, additional supporting evidence can be drawn from the accounts of the Battle of Gaugamela, where Arbela played a strategic role. Alexander the Great, recognizing the city's significance, made a decisive pilgrimage to the temple of Ishtar before his historic confrontation with Darius III. This act, which sought the blessing of the

Assyrian goddess, signified the city's persistent aura of sanctity and its perceived ability to sway the fortunes of empires.

In conclusion, the assertion that Arbela was a central pillar in the religious life of the Assyrian Empire is not only plausible but compelling. The city's temples, its rituals, and the fervent devotion of its inhabitants were not ephemeral expressions of faith but enduring symbols of an identity that withstood the vicissitudes of history. Arbela, in its quiet grandeur, was more than a city; it was a testament to the spiritual aspirations of a people who sought to anchor their earthly kingdom in the firmament of their gods.

Indeed, the stones of Arbela may no longer resound with the chants of worshipers, but their silence is eloquent. They beckon us to ponder the mysteries of faith and the indelible imprint it leaves on the canvas of history. Arbela stands, a hallowed ground that continues to whisper the secrets of a once-mighty empire, urging us to reflect on the enduring power of the sacred in shaping the human journey.

Assur: The Old Capital

ASSUR, THE VENERABLE heart of the ancient Assyrian Empire, rose from humble origins to become a city of monumental significance. Its journey through the corridors of time, from the administrative capital to a religious nexus, encapsulates the ebb and flow of Assyrian power and piety.

As we peel back the layers of history, it becomes apparent that Assur was more than a mere geographic location; it was a symbol of the empire's might and a custodian of its deepest spiritual yearnings. But what catalyzed this city's ascent to greatness? How did it evolve to command such reverence and influence across the Assyrian civilization and beyond?

Let us embark on a voyage through time, tracing the footsteps of Assur from its earliest origins to the echoes of its legacy that still resonate today.

Set against the backdrop of the Tigris River, the tale of Assur begins in an age shrouded by the mists of antiquity. Founded by a tapestry of tribes, the city's initial role was that of a modest trading outpost. Yet, the seeds of destiny were sown early, as the city took its name from the state god of Assyria, Assur, foreshadowing the profound bond between the divine and this nascent urban center.

As centuries turned like pages in a book, Assur's narrative saw the rise of formidable kings who spearheaded the expansion of the Assyrian Empire. Under their rule, the city transformed, its horizons broadening beyond commerce to become the beating heart of an empire. Magnificent palaces and temples soared towards the heavens, their imposing forms asserting the might of Assyrian kings.

But Assur's story is not one of unbroken glory. The city's fortunes waxed and waned with the tides of power, its prominence challenged by emerging urban centers like Nineveh and Nimrud. Yet, even as political preeminence shifted, Assur retained its spiritual gravitas, remaining a bastion of tradition and piety within the empire.

One might wonder, did the religious significance of Assur differ across the empire's expanse? Indeed, regional variations manifested in the form of local deities and customs, yet Assur maintained a unifying presence, a common thread binding the diverse tapestry of Assyrian beliefs.

As the centuries unfolded, newer chapters were added to Assur's chronicle. The city watched empires rise and fall, and yet it stood resilient, a steadfast sentinel of Assyrian heritage. The pivotal moment came with the invasion of the Babylonians and Medes, which saw the fall of the Assyrian Empire.

In the modern lens, Assur's silhouette is cast in a different light. Archaeologists and historians pore over its ruins, deciphering the stories etched into its relics. The modern world, with its keen eye for the past, has come to appreciate Assur's multifaceted legacy—from its architectural innovations to its contributions to art and literature.

Yet, the journey of Assur has not been without its controversies. Debates rage over the interpretation of texts and the chronology of events. Scholars contest the scale of its influence, dissecting the annals of history to distinguish fact from myth.

Assur stands at the crossroads of myth and history, a city that has captivated the imagination of generations.

Perhaps it is this very interplay of fact and fable that makes Assur's story so enduring, a narrative that invites us to reflect on the power of cities to shape the human experience.

Assur, the old capital, thus remains an indelible mark on the canvas of history, its legacy a testament to the grand aspirations of a civilization that sought to enshrine its identity in stone. In the silence of its ruins, we are urged to ponder: What legacies do we, the modern architects of civilization, wish to leave behind?

Innovations and Contributions

The Royal Library of Ashurbanipal

Imagine, if you will, an archive so vast and comprehensive that it encapsulated the pinnacle of ancient knowledge, an intellectual treasure trove that laid the foundations for the modern world's understanding of history, literature, science, and beyond. This is the story of how one king's insatiable thirst for knowledge led to the creation of a repository of wisdom so significant that its influence reverberates through the centuries.

Let us paint a picture of the Royal Library of Ashurbanipal, nestled within the bustling city of Nineveh, the heart of the Assyrian Empire. This was no ordinary collection of texts; it was the culmination of a monarch's ambition to assemble all the world's knowledge under his domain. Here, the meticulous work of scholars and scribes was conducted amidst walls lined with tens of thousands of clay tablets, each one a vessel carrying the precious cargo of human thought and understanding.

Have you ever wondered what it would be like to wander through such a place? To run your fingers across cuneiform inscriptions recounting epic tales, sophisticated medical treatises, and detailed astronomical observations? The library was a microcosm of the world, a place where scholars from diverse backgrounds gathered to share, debate, and expand the horizons of their wisdom.

But why should such ancient texts matter to us today? Consider for a moment the tale of Gilgamesh, an epic poem that grappled with the very essence of human existence—themes of life, death, and the search for immortality. This story, etched in clay, has transcended the ages, its narrative power undiminished by the passage of time. It serves as a testament to the universal human experience, a connection to our ancestors that remains startlingly relevant.

In the heart of the library, amidst the hush of scribes at work, an extraordinary level of detail was employed to ensure the longevity of knowledge. Can you picture the careful hands shaping the wet clay, the precision of the wedge-shaped script being pressed into its surface? This was a world where the value of knowledge was paramount, and its preservation was a sacred duty.

The Royal Library of Ashurbanipal was not merely a physical space; it was a beacon of culture and intellect, a symbol of the reverence for learning that characterized the Assyrian Empire.

Engineering Marvels

THE INGENUITY OF THE Assyrian Empire extended far beyond the literary treasures of the Royal Library of Ashurbanipal. As we shift our gaze from the papyrus and clay tablets to the stone and water, a different kind of legacy emerges—one of extraordinary engineering feats that showcase the sophistication, practicality, and foresight of Assyrian society. These marvels were not only functional but also symbolized the empire's might and advanced understanding of the world around them. Let us delve into the inventory of these achievements that stand as a testament to the empire's prowess.

The list that follows is not exhaustive but highlights the most significant engineering undertakings that have left an indelible mark on history.

Aqueducts and Water Management Systems

Imagine a vast network of channels and tunnels, intricately carved and constructed to harness the life-giving force of water across vast stretches of arid land. The Assyrians were pioneers in developing comprehensive water management systems, enabling them to irrigate crops, supply their cities, and maintain the splendor of their royal gardens.

The evidence of their mastery over hydraulic engineering is found in the remnants of their aqueducts, such as the one at Jerwan, built by King Sennacherib in the 7th century BCE. This aqueduct was part of a more extensive system designed to transport water from distant mountains to Nineveh, the empire's capital. The Jerwan Aqueduct, with its limestone blocks and precision-engineered gradient, stands as a symbol of Assyrian engineering acumen.

What's more, inscriptions on these aqueducts provide us with firsthand accounts of their construction, often detailing the number of workers, the time taken, and the challenges overcome. These records are invaluable, painting a vivid picture of the empire's capacity to mobilize resources and knowledge for grand-scale projects.

The practical applications of these water systems were manifold. They supported agriculture, which was the backbone of the Assyrian economy, and they also played a role in the empire's defense strategy. By controlling water sources, the Assyrians could fend off sieges, using water as both a protective moat and a means to sustain the population during prolonged attacks.

Monumental Architecture

Transitioning from the flow of water to the solidity of stone, the Assyrians were also master builders of monumental architecture. Their palaces and temples were not just places of residence and worship but also powerful symbols of political authority.

One cannot discuss Assyrian architecture without marveling at the grandeur of the palaces at Nimrud, Khorsabad, and Nineveh. The walls of these structures were lined with intricately carved stone reliefs depicting the king as a god-like figure, performing acts of valor and piety. These images were designed to inspire awe and ensure the king's legacy.

Archaeological digs have unearthed the foundations and layouts of these palaces, revealing a sophisticated understanding of spatial design and urban planning. The use of mud brick and stone, along with advanced construction techniques, allowed the Assyrians to create vast, imposing structures that stood firm against both the enemy and the elements.

The practical applications of these monumental structures were diverse. They served as administrative centers, housed royal courts, and acted as the stage for religious and ceremonial events. Their construction employed thousands, boosting the economy and displaying the might of the Assyrian kings to all who beheld them.

Systems of Governance

Behind every great engineering project lies an equally impressive system of governance. The Assyrian Empire was no exception, with its complex bureaucracy and well-defined roles that ensured the smooth execution of their engineering marvels.

The empire's administrative system was highly organized, with officials responsible for various aspects of construction, from resource allocation to labor management. This efficient bureaucracy was the engine that drove the empire's ability to conceive, construct, and maintain its engineering projects.

Evidence of this governance is found not only in the physical remnants of their achievements but also in the administrative records that have been preserved. These documents detail the logistics behind the empire's endeavors, from the distribution of rations to the assignment of work crews.

The practical application of these systems of governance extended to every corner of the empire. It allowed for the maintenance of public works, the collection of taxes, and the mobilization of armies. It was this structure that enabled the Assyrians to project their power and influence across the Near East.

The engineering marvels of the Assyrian Empire are a testament to their innovative spirit and enduring legacy. They harnessed the elements, erected structures of immense scale, and developed a governance system that brought these projects to fruition.

Bureaucratic Brilliance

IN THE SHADOW OF SUCH monumental architecture and intricate water systems, there lay the beating heart of the Assyrian Empire: its administrative system, an intricate web of order and efficiency that held the vast territories together like the sinews of a mighty beast. This network was not just a show of power but a sophisticated mechanism that managed an empire stretching from the Mediterranean to the heart of the Middle East. But within this brilliance, a significant issue lurked, threatening to unravel the tapestry of control the Assyrians had so masterfully woven.

As the empire expanded, the complexity of managing diverse cultures, languages, and vast distances presented a daunting challenge to the central authority. If left unchecked, this could lead to miscommunication, slow decision-making, and ultimately, the disintegration of the empire. The consequences of such administrative failure could be catastrophic, potentially leading to rebellions, economic collapse, and the loss of territories.

But the Assyrians, ever resourceful, developed a solution to this burgeoning problem. They created a system of provinces, each governed by a carefully selected official who reported directly to the king. These provincial governors were entrusted with the power to make decisions on behalf of the central authority, thus streamlining the bureaucratic process and ensuring swift action when needed.

To implement this solution, the empire was divided into smaller, more manageable provinces, each with its own administrative center. These centers were equipped with scribes, scholars, and local officials who were well-versed in the empire's laws and language, Akkadian. The provincial system was further bolstered by a network of roads and messengers, which facilitated quick communication between the provinces and the capital.

The efficacy of this solution is evident in the empire's longevity and its ability to maintain control over its territories. Records show that the Assyrians were able to swiftly mobilize resources and troops when faced with external threats, and effectively collect taxes and tributes to enrich the empire's coffers.

While the provincial system was the empire's primary strategy for maintaining its vast bureaucracy, alternative solutions were also in place. For instance, the use of spies and informants provided the king with a detailed understanding of the happenings within his empire, allowing for preemptive action against potential insurrections.

Furthermore, the Assyrians employed a merit-based promotion system within their bureaucracy, ensuring that the most capable individuals rose to power. This not only motivated officials to perform well but also ensured a high level of competence within the administrative ranks.

The brilliance of the Assyrian bureaucracy lay not only in its structure but also in its record-keeping. By maintaining detailed accounts of transactions, treaties, and decrees, the empire established a level of accountability and transparency that was unparalleled for its time. These records served as both a historical archive and a tool for governance, allowing for informed decisions based on past precedents.

As we marvel at the Assyrian Empire's bureaucratic brilliance, we must not forget that it was the foundation upon which their grand achievements were built. It was this invisible structure that enabled the visible wonders of the empire to exist. The Assyrians demonstrated that with a well-oiled administrative machine, even the most audacious feats of engineering and expansion are within reach.

Agricultural Advances

IN THE FERTILE CRESCENT of Mesopotamia, where the Tigris and Euphrates rivers swelled and receded with the changing seasons, the Assyrians embarked on a transformative journey. This was a path that would lead not only to securing food but also to the flourishing of a civilization. The goal was clear: revolutionize agriculture in a way that could sustain the ever-growing empire and cement its prosperity.

Before the Assyrians could reap the fruits of their labor, they needed to gather the seeds of innovation. The prerequisites were vast: an understanding of the land and climate; tools for tilling, sowing, and harvesting; systems for irrigation; and the domestication of crops and livestock. Only with these elements firmly in hand could they hope to transform the bare earth into a bountiful haven.

Imagine a tapestry of golden fields, the air filled with the scent of rich earth and ripening grain. In the broad overview, Assyrian agriculture was a symphony of interlocking steps: preparing the land, managing water resources, sowing seeds, tending to the growing plants, and finally, the harvest. Each phase was a note in the melody of cultivation, one that required precision and care to harmonize.

As we delve into the detailed steps, consider the plow as it breaks ground at dawn, the farmer guiding the oxen with a steady hand. The land was first tilled to aerate the soil, making it receptive to the seeds that would soon be sown. Following this, intricate channels and basins were constructed, harnessing the rivers' might to quench the thirsty crops. With a practiced rhythm, seeds were sown, each variety chosen for its suitability to the climate and its nutritional value.

Here, take heed of a few tips and warnings shared by the wise sages of the time: Rotate your crops to prevent soil depletion. Store your grain in elevated granaries to ward off moisture and pests. And most crucially, never leave a field fallow during the flood season, for that is when the soil is most fertile.

How does one verify that this agricultural revolution was a success? By the yield, of course. The Assyrians measured their success in the heft of their harvest baskets and the granaries that swelled with surplus. This surplus not only fed the populace but also supported trade, armies, and the splendor of the empire.

In the pursuit of agricultural excellence, challenges often arose. Pestilence could ravage a field, drought could wither the sprouts, and floods could be both a blessing and a curse. Yet, the Assyrians were adept troubleshooters. Crop rotation staved off the depletion and pests, while their advanced irrigation techniques mitigated the risks of both flood and drought.

Now, let us pause and ponder: How did the Assyrians view the earth beneath their feet? Was it merely a resource to be exploited, or did they see themselves as custodians of a precious gift? Their innovations in agriculture suggest a deep respect for the land that sustained them.

The use of iron in their tools—a luxury at the time—allowed for more efficient farming practices. Their intricate irrigation systems not only watered crops but also replenished the fertility of the soil. They showed us that with tenacity and insight, even the arid steppe could be coaxed into abundance.

In the silence that falls after the harvest, one can almost hear the whispers of Assyrian farmers sharing their stories. "See how the water flows just so," an elder might say, pointing to a perfectly graded canal. "And watch the way the barley heads nod when they're ready to be plucked from their stems," another would add with a knowing smile.

Who were these architects of abundance, these stewards of the soil? They were the unsung heroes of the Assyrian Empire, those whose calloused hands shaped the very foundation upon which an empire's greatness was built.

In our own times, with challenges of food security and sustainability looming large, there is wisdom to be gleaned from the Assyrian example.

They demonstrate that with foresight, innovation, and respect for the natural world, prosperity can be cultivated from the ground up.

As the sun sets on the Assyrian fields, casting long shadows over the neatly ordered rows of crops, let us remember that these agricultural advances were not just about feeding an empire. They were about creating a legacy that would endure through the ages, a testament to human ingenuity and the enduring bond between people and the land that nourishes them.

The Spread of Aramaic

IN THE WAKE OF ASSYRIAN agricultural prowess, a cultural phenomenon was simultaneously taking root—one that would eventually intertwine its way through the fabric of the Near East. The Assyrian Empire, ever-expanding, became the crucible within which the Aramaic language would find its voice, a voice that would echo across lands and through centuries.

Journey with me to the bustling streets of Nineveh, the heart of the empire, where traders from distant lands mingled with local scribes. It's the eighth century BCE, and a linguistic transformation is underway. Aramaic, once a modest language spoken by the Arameans, is on the cusp of becoming the lingua franca of an entire region.

What sparked this widespread adoption? The Assyrians, in their conquests, had amassed a vast territory, a mosaic of cultures and languages that demanded a common medium for administration and communication. Aramaic, with its flexible script and simplicity, proved to be the ideal candidate. It was the thread that could stitch together the empire's diverse tapestry.

As we trace the milestones in Aramaic's ascension, we witness its script being carved into the stone annals of history, its words shaping the trade agreements that crossed deserts, and its phrases whispered in the corridors of power. It was the merchant's haggle, the diplomat's treaty, and the proclamation of kings. How did this language, once confined to a small region, come to dominate such a grand stage?

Consider the caravans that traversed the Silk Road, carrying spices, textiles, and, unbeknownst to many, the seeds of cultural exchange. With each transaction and interaction, Aramaic planted its roots deeper into the soils of society. It became the conduit for commerce, a bridge for diplomacy, and a tool for governance.

Why does this matter in our modern world? Today, we live in a global village, where communication across cultures is vital. Understanding the spread of Aramaic sheds light on the power of language in uniting disparate peoples. It teaches us about adaptability, cultural exchange, and the enduring impact of connectivity.

Do you see the parallel lines of history? The internet, much like Aramaic then, now serves as the backbone of international communication. Just as Aramaic spread through trade routes and political power, digital languages traverse fiber-optic cables and satellite waves, binding the world in a network of shared understanding.

But let us not simply recount history; let us feel it. Imagine the scribe, his fingers stained with ink, as he transcribes an edict in the fluid Aramaic script. His work is not just clerical—it is the weaving of a linguistic bridge that will allow the Assyrian ruler's words to be understood across vast territories. Each stroke of his stylus is a testament to the power of language to transcend borders.

Who were the bearers of this linguistic torch? They were the merchants plying their trade on dusty roads, the scholars debating in academic forums, and the common folk recounting tales in the market squares. They carried the language from city to city, heart to heart, ensuring its legacy.

And now, as we stand at the threshold of the future, looking back at the past, we must ask ourselves: How do we honor the legacy of those who paved the way for our interconnected world? How do we ensure that our languages, tools of unity, are not turned into barriers?

Aramaic's influence is still palpable today. It can be found in the modern languages of the region, in religious texts, and in the cultural consciousness of the Near East. Its story is a reminder that the threads of history are woven not just by the hands of emperors and conquerors but also by the collective efforts of everyday people.

Empire at Its Zenith

The Reign of Tiglath-Pileser III

Throughout history, few figures loom as large as Tiglath-Pileser III, the king who redefined the Assyrian Empire and set the trajectory for its zenith. His reign marked an era of unparalleled transformation, one that would ripple through the ages and etch his name in the bedrock of ancient history.

The story of Tiglath-Pileser III, also known as Pul in biblical accounts, cannot be told without first stepping back to the earliest origins of the empire he would come to revolutionize. From the modest city-state that emerged in the heart of Mesopotamia, Assyria had grown by the time of his ascent to the throne in 745 BCE. The Assyrian kings before him had laid the groundwork, expanding the empire's reach through military conquests and strategic alliances.

Yet, it was under Tiglath-Pileser III that the empire underwent a metamorphosis that altered the very fabric of Near Eastern geopolitics. He ascended the throne during a time of turmoil, with the empire fraying at the edges, beset by internal strife and external threats. The king responded with a series of sweeping reforms that would not only stabilize his domain but also set the stage for an empire that would stretch from the Persian Gulf to the Mediterranean Sea.

His military campaigns were relentless and strategically masterful. In an unprecedented move, he reorganized the army into a standing force, making it a formidable tool for his ambitions. With this newly minted force, he subdued rebellious vassal states, integrated defeated enemies into the empire, and expanded its borders through swift and decisive campaigns.

But Tiglath-Pileser III's influence was not confined to the battlefield. He recognized the importance of a cohesive administrative system and implemented standardization across the empire. The introduction of Aramaic as the lingua franca served not only as a practical measure for communication but also as a cultural binder for the diverse subjects of his empire.

His reign also saw the rise of a sophisticated spy network and the use of propaganda to consolidate power. Intricate reliefs depicting his victories adorned the walls of his palaces, standing as silent yet potent declarations of his might and right to rule.

Can you imagine the awe of a subject, standing before such grandeur, understanding the might and reach of their ruler?

The empire's burgeoning economy and the revival of cities such as Kalhu (Nimrud) and Dur-Sharrukin (Khorsabad) owe much to his policies. Trade flourished under his rule, and the empire's wealth grew as it became the center of commerce in the ancient world.

Tiglath-Pileser III's impact on the regional and cultural variations within the empire was also significant. He pursued a policy of resettlement, moving conquered peoples across regions to quell nationalist sentiment and to blend the empire into a more unified entity. This melding of cultures, while sometimes brutal, contributed to a melting pot that would influence the region's identity for centuries.

In the modern narrative, Tiglath-Pileser III is often regarded as a pioneer of empire-building, a model for future leaders who sought to establish their own dominions. Historians and scholars dissect his strategies and governance, looking for insights into the art of statecraft and military tactics.

However, his reign was not without its challenges and controversies. The brutality of his campaigns and his harsh treatment of subjugated peoples have sparked debates among historians about the ethics of his methods. Furthermore, his death triggered a succession crisis that would test the resilience of the administrative and military structures he had so meticulously crafted.

In conclusion, the reign of Tiglath-Pileser III marked a turning point for the Assyrian Empire. His uncompromising vision and reforms laid the groundwork for a period of dominance that would see Assyria become the most powerful empire of its time. The echoes of his legacy, for better or for worse, continue to inform our understanding of the ancient Near East and the complex tapestry of human civilization.

Sargon II: The Empire Expands

IN THE SHADOW OF HIS predecessor's towering legacy, a new sovereign ascended to the throne of the Assyrian Empire. Sargon II, whose very name means "the legitimate king," would not only inherit the expansive domain shaped by Tiglath-Pileser III but also embark on his own ambitious journey to push the boundaries of Assyrian might further than ever before. This tale of conquest and empire is etched in history, a testament to Sargon II's drive to expand the empire's horizons.

The Assyrian Empire, though rooted deep in antiquity, found a new chapter with Sargon II. His reign, beginning in 722 BCE, unfolded at a time when the empire was already a formidable force in the ancient Near East. Yet, the stage was set for further expansion, and Sargon II rose to the challenge with a zeal that would cement his place in the annals of history.

Like the threads of a grand tapestry, the chronological sequence of significant events during Sargon II's reign tells a story of relentless ambition. He launched his first campaign shortly after taking the throne, quelling revolts and securing the borders. His military prowess became visible to all when he crushed the kingdom of Elam and subdued Urartu, extending Assyria's influence over new territories.

Imagine, if you will, the thunder of chariots and the clamor of battle as Sargon II led his army to victory after victory. Can you see the dust rising from the feet of soldiers as they march through conquered cities, erecting monuments to proclaim Assyrian dominance?

Stelae and reliefs from this period depict the grandeur of his military campaigns, showing the might of Assyrian warriors and the submission of their enemies.

The cultural and regional variations within the empire were further diversified under Sargon II's rule. He continued the policy of deporting and resettling conquered peoples, a strategy aimed at preventing uprisings and fostering cultural integration. This mixing of populations led to a rich blend of customs and traditions, which contributed to the Assyrian identity and the multilingual nature of its society.

In recent scholarship, Sargon II's reign has been reevaluated and appreciated for its contributions to the Assyrian Empire's administrative efficiency and military innovation. His development of the empire's infrastructure and his continuation of using Aramaic as the lingua franca solidified Assyria's position as a cultural and economic hub.

Yet, Sargon II's reign was not without its challenges and controversies. His military campaigns often involved significant destruction and forced population movements, raising questions about the humanitarian cost of his conquests. Additionally, the empire faced persistent resistance from both internal factions and external enemies, leading to a constant state of vigilance and military readiness.

The turning point came in 705 BCE, when Sargon II died on the battlefield, an unusual fate for an Assyrian king. His death ushered in a period of uncertainty, prompting questions about the stability and continuity of the empire he had worked so hard to expand.

In essence, Sargon II's reign marked a period of aggressive expansion and the consolidation of Assyrian power. His military achievements and administrative reforms furthered the empire's dominance in the Near East, leaving behind a legacy of might and ambition that would influence generations to come. The story of Sargon II, the king who boldly expanded the empire's boundaries, is a saga of power, innovation, and the timeless quest for glory.

Ashurbanipal: The Scholar King

IN THE HEART OF NINEVEH, under the shade of a sprawling palace garden, a young prince buried his head in the texts of old. This was no ordinary garden, and certainly, no ordinary boy. It was a sanctuary of knowledge, thoughtfully curated by the future king of Assyria, Ashurbanipal. Unlike the gardens that merely boasted of earthly delights, this place was a paradise for the mind, a testament to a ruler whose passion for wisdom equaled his hunger for power.

Ashurbanipal, a name that would echo through the corridors of time, was not merely an inheritor of the Assyrian throne but a harbinger of a cultural renaissance that would immortalize his reign. His passion for collecting texts from across his vast empire revealed a king who sought to conquer not just lands but the realms of knowledge and understanding.

The sun cast long shadows over the scholars who frequented the garden, their conversations a blend of philosophy, science, and poetry. The prince, a beacon of curiosity among them, listened intently, absorbing every word like a sponge. His disposition was a mirror to his future self—both a warrior and a learned man, embodying the duality of his empire's might and intellectual ambitions.

As the narrative of the garden scene unfolds, we peer into Ashurbanipal's soul, witnessing the internal struggle of a man who was both a product and a shaper of his time. He was the epitome of the Assyrian ideal—powerful and enlightened, a ruler who could discuss the intricacies of administration and recite epic poetry with equal finesse.

The tranquility of the garden was often disrupted by the news of skirmishes and rebellions, a reminder of the unpredictable world Ashurbanipal was destined to rule. Each report was a thread in the tapestry of his burgeoning empire, each decision a stroke of the brush that painted his legacy.

Isn't it remarkable how a single life can encapsulate the spirit of an age? Ashurbanipal's story is not just a tale of Assyrian grandeur but a reflection of humanity's enduring quest for understanding. He was a man who believed that the truest form of power lay not in subjugation but in the enlightenment of his people.

As readers, we stand at the threshold of wisdom, about to traverse the halls of Ashurbanipal's famed library. There, amidst clay tablets inscribed with cuneiform, we find the collective knowledge of ancient civilizations. This was his gift to posterity—a library that would survive the ebb and flow of empires, preserving knowledge that might have otherwise been lost to the sands of time.

Why did Ashurbanipal devote himself to such a monumental task? Was it a desire for immortality, a way to etch his name into the bedrock of history? Or was it something purer—a genuine yearning to understand the world and share that understanding with all who would come after?

Consider the implications of such an endeavor. In a world where might was right, Ashurbanipal's library was a beacon of enlightenment. It was not only a repository of texts but a symbol of the cultural diversity and intellectual pursuits that flourished under his reign. The library housed astronomical treatises, medical texts, and legal codes, reflecting a society that valued knowledge as a cornerstone of civilization.

Through the lens of history, Ashurbanipal's passion for learning seems almost prophetic. By fostering a culture of intellectual inquiry, he sowed the seeds for advancements that would benefit not just Assyria but all of humanity. His dedication to the arts and sciences was a declaration that the empire's strength was rooted in more than just military prowess—it was anchored in the collective wisdom of its people.

Ashurbanipal's reign was not without its shadows, for no empire can rise without casting darkness upon some. Yet, in the grand narrative of

Assyrian history, his contributions to culture and knowledge shine as a legacy that transcends the ages.

How, then, shall we remember this scholar king? As a conqueror with a thirst for wisdom? As a patron of the arts, who understood that the true measure of a civilization lies in its contributions to human progress? Or perhaps, as a visionary, who recognized that the greatest empires are built not just on the might of armies but on the power of ideas?

The story of Ashurbanipal is not merely a chapter in the annals of the Assyrian Empire. It is a tale of the universal human spirit, of our relentless pursuit of knowledge and the desire to leave a lasting mark on the world. It is an invitation to embark on an unexpected journey through time, to discover the wisdom that lies hidden in the past, and to glean insights that illuminate our path forward.

Assyria's International Influence

IN THE SHADOW OF ASHURBANIPAL'S scholarly pursuits, the Assyrian Empire wielded a cultural and technological prowess that resonated far beyond the reaches of its political borders. The influence of Assyria on neighboring civilizations was not merely a byproduct of its military conquests but a deliberate export of culture, governance, and innovation. As we peel back the layers of history, we uncover the subtle, yet profound impact of Assyrian civilization on its contemporaries.

Why did the Assyrians, formidable in their might, invest in the intricate tapestry of international influence? Perhaps it was a testament to their understanding of the power of cultural hegemony, where the pen and the sword were equally mighty in carving realms. The comparison of Assyrian influence with that of neighboring empires offers us a panoramic view of ancient geopolitics.

To establish a framework for this analysis, we consider three main criteria: cultural exports, technological advancements, and administrative practices. These benchmarks will serve as our navigational stars as we voyage through the ancient world, charting the similarities and contrasts in the international influence wielded by the Assyrians and their peers.

The cultural exports of the Assyrian Empire were both vast and varied. Similar to the way Hellenistic culture spread through Alexander's conquests, Assyrian art, language, and religion permeated the fabric of societies within their sphere of control. The omnipresence of the Akkadian language, the lingua franca of the empire, facilitated not only governance but also the diffusion of ideas across the Fertile Crescent. This mirrors the later proliferation of Greek and Latin in their respective empires, though contrasted by the Assyrian penchant for incorporating the deities of subjugated peoples into their own pantheon—an example of cultural assimilation that underscored a nuanced approach to empire-building.

Technological advancements were another domain where Assyria's influence shone. The empire's engineers revolutionized warfare with the introduction of iron weaponry and siege equipment, innovations that neighboring civilizations were quick to adopt and adapt. Their irrigation systems and public works inspired urban planning across the region. While other civilizations also contributed significantly to technological progress, the Assyrian approach was marked by a relentless pursuit of efficiency that often turned the tide of battle and reshaped the landscape of urban life.

In governance, the Assyrians introduced a systematic approach to administration and law enforcement that echoed in the corridors of power from Babylon to Persia. The use of a network of governors and a standing army ensured a tight grip on the empire's vast territories, a concept that was emulated by successive empires. The contrast here is stark when juxtaposed with the more decentralized governance seen in some of their contemporaries, highlighting the Assyrian preference for control and order.

Visual aids, such as comparative charts or maps, would be instrumental in illustrating these points, but let us not forget the power of the written word to paint a picture in the mind's eye. Imagine the Assyrian influence as a river, its tributaries reaching into every aspect of neighboring societies, nourishing some areas while reshaping others.

The broader implications of these comparisons are as rich as the fertile soil of Mesopotamia. They reveal an empire that understood the strength derived from cultural cohesion, the strategic advantage of technological superiority, and the stabilizing force of unified governance. In essence, the Assyrian influence set a precedent for what it meant to be an international power in the ancient world.

How does this ancient tale of influence resonate today? The legacy of the Assyrians can be seen in modern governance, military strategy, and even in the way cultures interact and blend on the global stage. The principles of administration and law that were refined in the Assyrian courts find echoes in the corridors of contemporary power.

The Assyrian Empire, in its quest for dominion, sowed seeds of culture, technology, and governance that would sprout across the ages, influencing civilizations long after its demise. Was it their intention to leave such an indelible mark, or was it the unintended consequence of empire? Such questions invite us to ponder the ripples of our actions through the annals of time.

As we consider the intricacies of Assyrian influence, we are compelled to recognize the duality of their legacy—a blend of enlightenment and subjugation that has been the hallmark of empires throughout history. In the grand narrative, the Assyrian Empire stands as a colossus, its shadow falling on both the pages of history and the unwritten future.

Let us then, with a discerning eye, examine the remnants of Assyria's international influence, for in understanding the past, we may yet glean wisdom that lights the path of our collective journey. As the echoes of Assyria's grandeur still reverberate, we are reminded of the enduring power of culture and innovation to transcend borders and epochs, shaping the world in ways both seen and unseen.

The Wealth of Nations

THE ASSYRIAN EMPIRE was sustained not just by the might of its warriors but by the wealth that flowed into its coffers through tribute, trade, and economic acumen. A canvas of commerce and coercion painted the landscape of this ancient superpower, where the accumulation of wealth was as strategic as the deployment of armies.

Against the backdrop of a burgeoning empire, the Assyrians crafted a sophisticated system of tribute and taxation that underpinned their economic strength. The conquered territories, integrated into the imperial fold, were not merely subdued but were transformed into vital arteries of wealth, pumping resources and riches back to the heart of the empire.

The central figures in this economic tour de force were the Assyrian kings, who wielded absolute power and were considered the earthly representatives of the gods. They were supported by a cadre of officials and merchants, the unsung heroes of the empire's economic machinery. These individuals, adept in the art of negotiation and ruthless in the extraction of wealth, ensured a steady flow of tribute and trade.

The challenge for the Assyrians was not only to conquer but to maintain a firm grip on disparate lands, each with its unique resources and potential for rebellion. The empire's answer to this problem was multifaceted: a blend of military intimidation, diplomatic maneuvering, and strategic marriages.

The approach to extracting tribute was methodical and relentless. Conquered kings were compelled to pay homage to their Assyrian overlords, often in the form of gold, silver, and other precious commodities. But Assyria's economic strategy extended beyond mere extortion. They facilitated trade networks that spanned the known world, connecting the Mediterranean to the Persian Gulf. Assyrian merchants acted as intermediaries in the exchange of goods such as textiles, tin, and luxury items, amassing wealth through tariffs and trade deals.

The results of these strategies were staggering. The empire amassed wealth on a scale unprecedented in the ancient Near East. The splendor of the Assyrian capitals—Nineveh, Ashur, and Nimrud—was funded by this influx of wealth. Palaces adorned with intricate reliefs and colossal statues, and grandiolesque gardens, such as the fabled Hanging Gardens, were testaments to the empire's prosperity.

An analysis of these economic policies reveals a shrewd understanding of power dynamics. The Assyrians knew that wealth could buy loyalty or, at the very least, compliance. They leveraged their economic strength to solidify their political dominance and to fund the expansion of their military machine.

Connecting these economic threads to the larger narrative of the Assyrian Empire's success reveals a clear picture: wealth was both a means and an end. The accumulation of riches was integral to the empire's ability to project power and maintain stability within its vast territories.

However, as the twilight of the empire approached, the wealth of the Assyrians could not stave off the decline brought on by overextension and internal strife.

The Decline and Fall

Internal Decay

The Assyrian Empire, a titan of the ancient world, was not felled by a single blow from an external force but was instead eroded by a trifecta of social, political, and economic factors that conspired to weaken its foundations. The very fabric that held the empire together began to unravel, as the strength that once intimidated nations became the harbinger of its downfall.

Imagine, if you will, a society where the divide between the elite and the common folk grew so vast that it became a chasm, where the opulence of the few stood in stark contrast to the poverty of the many. This disparity sowed the seeds of discontent, breeding resentment and eroding the trust and loyalty that had once been the empire's bulwark.

Consider the tale of Ninurta, a once-loyal soldier in the Assyrian army, whose story mirrors the plight of many. Ninurta, who had fought valiantly for his king, returned home to find his family's land seized by a corrupt official, his pleas for justice falling on deaf ears. His loyalty turned to bitterness, and bitterness to rebellion. Ninurta's story is but one thread in a tapestry of grievances that wove a narrative of dissatisfaction and disloyalty across the empire.

As the social fabric tore, so too did the political integrity of the empire. Power became increasingly centralized, with a succession of rulers who viewed dissent as a threat to be crushed rather than a symptom of deeper malaise. The royal court, once a place of counsel and collaboration, became an echo chamber where the whispers of conspiracy replaced the voices of reason. Corruption infected the highest echelons, with officials more concerned with lining their pockets than with the welfare of the state.

And what of the economy, the lifeblood of any civilization? The Assyrian economy, overly reliant on conquest and tribute, proved unsustainable. As the empire expanded, the cost of maintaining its territories and armies ballooned, while the influx of wealth and slaves from conquered lands disrupted local economies and labor systems.

Can you grasp the gravity of such a situation? The empire, once a beacon of strength and prosperity, was buckling under its own weight, its glories predicated on a fragile foundation that could not endure the test of time.

The Rise of New Powers

IN THE SHADOW OF THE mighty Assyrian Empire, once deemed invincible with its formidable cities and indomitable armies, a stirring began. Who could have predicted that the Medes, Babylonians, and Scythians would rise from obscurity to challenge Assyria's supremacy? Yet, history is often a testament to the unforeseen, to the undercurrents that shift the balance of power with the subtlety of a whisper before roaring into the cacophony of change.

It was amidst this restless epoch that new powers emerged, reshaping the ancient Near East. How did these nascent states rise to prominence, and what were the ramifications of their ascent for the Assyrian behemoth?

Let us begin our tale in the lands that cradled civilization, where the earliest origins of these emerging powers lay buried beneath the annals of time. The Medes, dwelling in the mountainous regions of what is now Iran, were initially a confederation of tribes, their collective might yet to be harnessed. The Babylonians, inheritors of the storied legacy of Sumer and Akkad, bided their time by the fertile banks of the Euphrates.

Meanwhile, the enigmatic Scythians roamed the vast steppes of Eurasia, their nomadic lifestyle veiling their potential for disruption.

As the sun traced its path across the sky, so too did these cultures evolve, their major milestones marking the passage from obscurity to eminence. Medes united under powerful kings, forging an identity that transcended tribal lines. In Babylon, the ascent of leaders like Nabopolassar signaled a resurgence of power and ambition. The Scythians, with their mastery of horseback warfare, became a force to be reckoned with, their raids sending tremors through the settled empires to their south.

Imagine now, if you can, the sight of the Medes' fortified capitals, their walls standing as a testament to a newfound sense of permanence and strength.

These cultures, though sharing the common goal of challenging Assyrian dominance, were as varied as the landscapes they inhabited. The Medes developed administrative systems that allowed for centralized control, while the Babylonians, steeped in the traditions of Mesopotamian civilization, cultivated scholarly and religious institutions. The Scythians, in contrast, maintained a decentralized society where tribal leaders held sway, their culture woven into the fabric of their nomadic lifestyle.

What then, were the modern interpretations or adaptations of these ancient peoples? Today, the Medes are often seen as forerunners to the vast Persian Empire that would later dominate the region. The legacy of Babylonian science, mathematics, and law can be found in much of our own cultural bedrock. As for the Scythians, they are sometimes depicted as the archetypal horse-riding warriors of antiquity, their influence perceived in various nomadic groups that followed.

But no historical narrative is without its challenges and controversies. Were the Medes truly a unified force, or was their cohesion exaggerated by ancient historians? Did the Babylonians innovate, or did they simply inherit? How did the Scythians maintain their independence despite the pressures of settled empires? These are the turning points, the subjects of fierce debate among scholars, and they serve to remind us that history is not a static tableau but a dynamic conversation across the ages.

As we delve deeper into the fabric of this era, a tapestry of conflict and conquest emerges. The Medes, under leaders like Cyaxares, reformed their army, adopting innovations such as the division of troops into specialized units. This military restructuring allowed them to engage more effectively with the Assyrians and later, the Lydians, altering the balance of power in the region.

Babylon, reinvigorated under the rule of Nabopolassar and his son Nebuchadnezzar II, embarked on campaigns that slowly chipped away at Assyria's might. The famed city of Nineveh fell to a combined force of Medes, Babylonians, and others in 612 BCE, a date that reverberates as a death knell for Assyrian dominance.

And what of the Scythians? Their incursions into the Near East were not conquests in the traditional sense but rather raids that siphoned the strength of the Assyrian periphery, adding to the strain on an empire overstretched.

In remembering the rise of these new powers, we must ask ourselves: What lessons do they impart? Can we draw parallels with emerging states in our modern world, with the shifting sands of power that continue to define our geopolitical landscape?

Beneath the shadow of the past, we recognize the whispers of our own time, the constant ebb and flow of empires and nations. The rise of the Medes, Babylonians, and Scythians serves as a powerful reminder that no empire is eternal, that the currents of time will always bring forth new powers to challenge the established order.

The Fall of Nineveh

AS DAWN BROKE OVER the ancient city of Nineveh, a sense of foreboding hung in the air. This once-thriving capital, a jewel of the

Assyrian Empire, now lay under the shadow of its imminent demise. The year was 612 BCE, and the relentless siege engines of a formidable alliance—Medes, Babylonians, and their confederates—were poised to breach the city's vaunted walls. One could almost hear the whispers of the citizens within, their voices a blend of prayer and despair, as the end of an era loomed.

This siege was not the beginning of Assyria's troubles, but the culmination of a series of events that heralded the fall of an empire that had once stretched from the Mediterranean to the heart of Mesopotamia. The Assyrians had ruled with an iron fist, their reputation for brutality both awe-inspiring and terrifying. But as the saying goes, the taller they stand, the harder they fall. Who could have imagined that the Assyrian Empire, which had once made the very earth tremble, now stood on the brink of annihilation?

The Assyrian military machine, renowned for its ferocity and tactical prowess, had faltered. Its enemies, once disparate and disorganized, had found unity in their common cause: to bring down the oppressor. The Medes had grown in power under the astute leadership of Cyaxares, who transformed their military into a force capable of standing toe-to-toe with Assyria's legions. Babylon, under Nabopolassar, had risen from Assyria's shadow, its resurgence fueled by a potent combination of military strength and shrewd diplomacy.

Yet, why does this ancient conquest matter to the contemporary reader? Why should the dust of Nineveh's ruins concern us now? Let's ponder for a moment the fate of empires, the rise and fall that seems an immutable rhythm of history. The modern world, much like the ancient, is a mosaic of nations and states, each vying for power, influence, and survival. The story of Nineveh's fall serves as a stark reminder that no power is invincible, no reign absolute. It is a lesson in the impermanence of dominance and the cycle of history that seems to repeat itself with each passing age.

But let us delve deeper, past the surface lessons of power and its fleeting nature, into the heart of the human experience. Picture the scenes within the besieged city: the fear in the eyes of a child, the resolve of a soldier manning the battlements for the final time, the desperation of leaders trying to maintain order amidst chaos. These are the moments that transcend time, the visceral human elements that connect us across millennia.

The siege of Nineveh stands as a testament to the inevitability of change. Ancient texts speak of the ferocity with which the allied forces attacked and the relentless defense mounted by the Assyrians. The city, once a bastion of culture and learning, crumbled under the onslaught, its vast libraries and palaces consumed by flames.

How did it come to this? Was it merely the military prowess of Assyria's enemies, or were there deeper fractures within the empire itself? Scholars suggest that internal strife, economic troubles, and the overextension of resources all played a part in weakening the once-mighty empire. These internal issues, perhaps overlooked by the Assyrian rulers in their hubris, were as much a cause of their downfall as the swords and spears of their adversaries.

The fall of Nineveh was not merely an end but a beginning. It signaled the birth of new powers, the reshaping of the Near Eastern political landscape, and the dawning of an era that would see the rise of new empires, each with their own stories of ascendancy and decline. As we close this chapter on Assyria, let us carry its lessons forward, embracing the past not as a distant relic but as a living, breathing guide to navigating the complexities of our world.

Nineveh fell, but from its ashes rose a tapestry of human endeavor that continues to unfold. Through the lens of history, we gain perspective, understanding, and perhaps a measure of foresight. The echoes of the past resonate, and it is our task to listen, to learn, and to remember.

Last Stand at Harran

WHISPERS OF THE PAST still lingered in the air as the once-mighty Assyrian Empire faced its twilight. The fall of Nineveh had not been the final death knell; a remnant of the once indomitable force gathered for one last stand. It was in the year 609 BCE, against the backdrop of a sun-scorched landscape, that the proud city of Harran held the last embers of Assyrian resistance.

In the heart of ancient Mesopotamia, where the Balikh River joins the Euphrates, lay Harran, a city of strategic importance and the last stronghold of the Assyrians. With its ancient temple dedicated to the moon god Sin, Harran was more than a city; it was a symbol of Assyrian resilience, a beacon of hope for a revival that was never to be.

The key figures at this juncture were the beleaguered King Ashur-uballit II, rallying his forces to reclaim the glory of his ancestors, and the mighty Babylonian king Nabopolassar, whose armies, allied with the Medes, stood confident and resolute, aiming to extinguish Assyria's final flame.

The challenge was formidable: a weakened Assyria, its military might shattered, its people demoralized, sought to fend off a relentless enemy. The problem was not just one of military strategy but of survival itself, for the very identity of an empire was at stake.

Ashur-uballit II mustered what was left of his army, bolstering his ranks with mercenaries and calling upon the aid of the Egyptians, whose pharaoh, Necho II, was sympathetic to his cause. The strategy was clear: defend Harran at all costs, and with Egyptian reinforcements, counterattack and reclaim lost territories.

The results, however, were grim. Harran fell in 609 BCE, despite the Assyrians' valiant efforts. The city was taken by the Babylonians, and the Assyrian king was forced to flee, his dreams of empire shattered. The once-great Assyrian military machine could not withstand the combined might of its adversaries.

In retrospect, the fall of Harran was not just the result of military defeat but also the culmination of a series of missteps and oversights by the Assyrian leadership. The overreliance on brute force, the failure to adapt to changing political landscapes, and the neglect of internal reforms all contributed to the empire's downfall.

The siege of Harran was not an isolated event but a part of the larger narrative of the Assyrian Empire's decline. It was a testament to the transient nature of power and the relentless march of time that spares no civilization, no matter how grand.

As the sun set on the once-mighty Assyrian Empire, one is left to ponder: What becomes of a civilization when its time has passed? Do the echoes of its greatness fade into oblivion, or do they serve as a cautionary tale for future generations?

The story of Harran, while a tale of defeat and despair, also serves as a beacon for those who study the past. It is a poignant reminder that the mightiest of empires are not immune to the ravages of time and the shifting sands of fate. As history's pages turn, the legacy of the Assyrian Empire—its innovations, its art, and its indomitable spirit—continues to inform and inspire.

Let us not forget Harran, nor the lessons it imparts. In the annals of history, it stands not merely as a city that fell but as a symbol of a civilization's enduring will to survive against all odds. The Assyrian Empire may have crumbled, but its story remains a testament to the complex tapestry of human achievement.

In the shadow of Harran's walls, we reflect on the inexorable cycle of rise and fall that marks the passage of empires. As students of history, we are reminded that our own civilization, no matter how advanced, is but a single thread in the ever-unfolding fabric of time.

What, then, can we learn from the last stand at Harran? How can we ensure that the lessons of the past are not forgotten but serve as guideposts for our future? These are the questions that linger, prompting us to delve deeper into the study of history, to unravel the complex web of human endeavor, and to seek understanding in the stories of those who came before us.

The echoes of Assyria's fall at Harran reverberate through time, a haunting reminder of the fragility of empires and the enduring quest for legacy. Let us listen to these echoes, learn from them, and continue the never-ending pursuit of knowledge that history so generously provides.

Note to the reader

Dear Readers,

Thank you for taking the time to read this exciting true story about the Assyrian Empire. I invite you to share your thoughts and reflections through a review. Whether you found a particular chapter enlightening, a narrative captivating, or have constructive feedback to offer, your insights are immensely valuable to me. Reviews not only help other readers in their decision to explore the depths of history but also provide me with invaluable feedback to enhance future editions. If you're passionate about history and would like to dive deeper into discussions, consider joining my review team on Booksprout. Together, we can uncover the hidden gems of the past and continue to illuminate the paths of knowledge. Thank you for your support and for embarking on this historical journey with me.

Warm regards,
History Nerds

Don't miss out!

Visit the website below and you can sign up to receive emails whenever History Nerds publishes a new book. There's no charge and no obligation.

https://books2read.com/r/B-A-ODOK-RVRVC

BOOKS 2 READ

Connecting independent readers to independent writers.

Also by History Nerds

Ancient Empires
The Ottoman Empire
Rome: The Rise and Fall
The Mongol Empire
The Assyrian Empire

Celtic Heroes and Legends
Celtic History
William Butler Yeats: Nobel Prize Winning Poet
Robert the Bruce
Scáthach
Finn McCool
William Wallace: Scotland's Great Freedom Fighter

Frauen des Krieges
Boudica: Königin der Icener
Jeanne d'Arc
Irena Sendler

Great Wars of the World
World War 1
World War 2
The Napoleonic Wars: One Shot at Glory
The Serbian Revolution: 1804-1835
Peace Won by the Saber: The Crimean War, 1853-1856
The Fiery Maelstrom of Freedom
The Wars of the Roses

Pirate Chronicles
Grace O'Malley: The Pirate Queen of Ireland
Blackbeard
William Kidd
Ching Shih

The History of the Vikings
Vikings
Longships on Restless Seas

Women of War
Boudica: Queen of the Iceni
Joan of Arc
Irena Sendler
Virginia Hall
Queen Amanirenas

World History
The History of the United Kingdom
The History of Ireland
The History of America
The History of Scotland
The History of Wales

Standalone
Grace O'Malley: Die Piratenkönigin von Irland